leonardo dicaprio
MODERN-DAY ROMEO

D1332850

leonardo dicaprio
MODERN-DAY ROMEO

BY GRACE CATALANO

BANTAM BOOKS
TORONTO · NEW YORK · LONDON · SYDNEY · AUCKLAND

LEONARDO DICAPRIO:
MODERN-DAY ROMEO
A BANTAM BOOK : 0 553 50663 3

First published in the USA by Bantam Doubleday
Dell Books For Young Readers
First publication in Great Britain

PRINTING HISTORY
Bantam edition published 1997
Reprinted 1998 (twice)
Updated edition reissued 1998
All rights reserved

Condition of Sale

Bantam Books are published by Transworld Publishers Ltd,
61–63 Uxbridge Road, London W5 5SA,
in Australia by Transworld Publishers (Australia) Pty Ltd,
15–25 Helles Avenue, Moorebank, NSW 2170,
and in New Zealand by Transworld Publishers (NZ) Ltd,
3 William Pickering Drive, Albany, Auckland.

Printed and bound in Great Britain by
Cox & Wyman Ltd, Reading, Berkshire.

To Rose and Sam

I couldn't have done it without you.
Thanks for everything!

CONTENTS

CONTENTS

Acknowledgments

The author would like to thank Joseph Catalano for his incredible help on this book. Thanks also to Grace Palazzo, Ralph J. Miele, Mary Michaels, and Jane Burns.

Special thanks to Beverly Horowitz, Karen Meyers, and everyone who worked on this book at Bantam Doubleday Dell.

And all my love to my parents, Rosemarie and Salvatore, who continue to support me!

leonardo dicaprio

MODERN-DAY ROMEO

chapter 1

SILVER SCREEN DREAM

Leonardo DiCaprio is the most riveting and sought-after new actor in Hollywood. From the moment he appeared on the big screen, the camera loved him. With his piercing blue-green eyes and his shock of blond hair, Leonardo is breaking hearts *and* box office records around the globe.

In less than five years, he has established himself as a major player in the Hollywood game—and he is only just beginning. At twenty-three years old, with a handful of films to his credit, Leonardo continues to prove how talented he is over and over. His performances garner glowing reviews. At only nineteen, he received an Academy Award nomination for his touching portrayal of Arnie, Johnny Depp's mentally impaired younger brother, in the extraordinary film *What's Eating Gilbert Grape*.

Leonardo has won the adoration of

thousands of fans as well as the admiration of his peers. Everyone gushes over his acting—critics, directors, and his costars.

Gilbert Grape director Lasse Hallström says, "I am convinced Leonardo is star material."

Michael Caton-Jones, who directed Leonardo in *This Boy's Life*, says, "He is a really brave actor. He'll do intelligent material with depth, feeling, and range, but he'll also have a lot of sex appeal. I saw his performance in *What's Eating Gilbert Grape*. That's what separates movie stars from everyday actors, the ability to take a flying moment of madness."

Sharon Stone, Leonardo's costar in *The Quick and the Dead*, gave up part of her salary so that Leonardo could join the cast. "He is the most gifted young actor I have ever seen," she says.

Leonardo's performances reveal an amazing depth that sets him apart from most other young actors. In fact, many people who saw his performance as Arnie in *Gilbert Grape* thought the character was actually played by a mentally impaired boy—*not* an actor.

Leonardo is a photographer's dream. When he looks into a camera, a transformation takes place. One cameraman who worked with him says, "He looks great in any light and from every angle. You can put him under fluorescent lighting and he still looks like a million dollars."

With his easygoing, fun-loving attitude, Leonardo plays the most difficult roles effortlessly. He has such a natural style that it's easy to forget he's acting. He exudes both magnetism and sensitivity onscreen, a devastating combination. And he has deliberately accepted a variety of unlikely and interesting roles—from a French poet to a heroin addict—rather than taking easy parts in surefire box office hits.

What is most interesting about Leonardo is that he is not a manufactured star, one pumped out of some publicity machine. He got where he is on his own, just by believing in his acting and proving to others he was capable of playing diverse characters. He himself decided to tackle this career and see how far he could get.

Leonardo is the first to admit that he is surprised by his quick success. When he set out to become an actor, he had no burning ambition to transform into a movie star. As a child, he would go to Robert De Niro or Al Pacino films and imagine himself playing their roles. "I never really took it seriously," he says. "I never really thought it would happen."

But it *has* happened, and now that

Leonardo has become the most in-demand young actor in Hollywood, he is enjoying every minute of it.

At the same time, Leonardo is anxious about his future and careful about the parts he takes. He is constantly looking for roles that will challenge him and help him to grow as an actor. He's not afraid to take chances with his career. And he doesn't care how much money people offer him—he will not do a movie he doesn't believe in.

"I think people expected me to go a certain way with my career, and I didn't do it," he says. "I didn't do the next John Grisham movie. I want to keep doing different things. I want to try everything, as long as it's real."

It is daring for a young actor to accept unconventional roles and do the unexpected. Leonardo believes in shaking things up and doing work that, in the end, will last a long time and will matter.

One role that mattered a great deal to Leonardo was Romeo in the exhilarating updated *William Shakespeare's Romeo & Juliet*. "At first I wasn't sure about doing it," he says. "I didn't want to run around in tights swinging a sword around. But Baz (Baz Luhrmann, the film's director, writer, and producer) convinced me to come to Australia and meet with him for a week, and while I was there he figured out what his vision was, and then I was really interested."

Leonardo was Baz Luhrmann's one and only choice to play Romeo. Luhrmann became aware of the young actor after seeing his photo in a magazine. "He was at a social event, and the caption read '... and of course, there's *that* actor,' " says Luhrmann. "I didn't realize that he had just been nominated for an Academy Award. I wondered what they meant by '*that* actor.' I thought, *Either he's really good or he's done something infamous.* When I later came to know him, I found that he was capable of both. I thought that Leonardo was an extraordinary young actor, and I thought he'd make a great Romeo. It's important to reveal these eternal characters anew for every generation, and Leonardo is particularly suited for this. He does seem to symbolize his generation. I just thought he'd be a perfect Romeo; it was as simple as that."

Luhrmann was right on target in casting Leonardo as Romeo opposite the equally talented Claire Danes as Juliet.

When the reviews for the film came in, they were glowing. Critics praised the film and Leonardo, calling him "an ardent Romeo, sensitive, brave, delicately hunky." *The New York Post* declared, "DiCaprio throws himself into the role but not over a cliff. He is Romeo."

Time magazine said the film was "a *Rebel Without a Cause* for the '90s," while *Rolling Stone* wrote, "DiCaprio and Danes fill their classic roles with vital passion. Shakespeare has never been this sexy onscreen."

As if that film wasn't enough to guarantee Leonardo's star status in Hollywood, he followed it up with another powerful performance. He starred in *Marvin's Room* opposite veteran actors Meryl Streep, Robert De Niro, and Diane Keaton. Next, of course, he triumphed in James Cameron's smash-hit epic, *Titanic.* There is definitely no stopping Leonardo DiCaprio.

Despite his talent, global fame, and celebrated good looks, Leonardo remains one of Hollywood's most enigmatic actors. He's on a fast track to becoming one of the biggest stars of our time, but he seems completely unfazed by all the attention.

We've seen Leonardo in a wide array of roles, but very little has been written about his life offscreen. Who is Leonardo DiCaprio? Where did he come from? How does he feel about his amazing rise to stardom? You're about to find out!

chapter 2

A Star Is Born

Leonardo's parents, George DiCaprio and Irmelin Idenbirken, met in college. Irmelin had moved to the United States from Germany as a young girl. When the two met, it was love at first sight. George and Irmelin shared the same interests and dreams and felt ready to settle down and start raising a family. Without much money, they moved to Los Angeles.

On November 11, 1974, their only child, Leonardo Wilhelm DiCaprio, was born. They named him after the Renaissance artist Leonardo Da Vinci. While she was looking at a Da Vinci painting in a museum in Italy, Irmelin felt her unborn baby kick. That, and the fact that Leonardo's paternal grandfather's middle name was Leon, clinched the decision.

For the first year of baby Leonardo's life, everything in the DiCaprio household seemed perfect. George and Irmelin thought they were ready for the responsibility of raising a child. But they were young, and it proved to be too much for them. Even though they adored their baby boy, George and Irmelin separated when Leonardo was only one year old.

During this difficult time, Irmelin sent her baby off on a Russian cruise ship with her parents. While Leonardo was on his first vacation, Irmelin and George split up their belongings and moved into separate homes. They vowed to stay friends, and to both be there for their baby.

After his parents went their separate ways, Leonardo lived primarily with his mother. But his father, who moved just across Los Angeles, was always around to spend time with his young son. Over the years, George made sure he spent many hours at Leonardo and Irmelin's home, trying to give his son a stable background and helping to raise him.

"George and I have always spent a lot of time together with Leonardo," says Irmelin. "While he was growing up, we always had dinner together and took him out to amusement parks and movies."

Irmelin explains that Leonardo found the arrangement at home very normal. "It never really seemed like George wasn't there for Leonardo because there was constant communication. Although his dad wasn't physically in the house at night, during the day he was there."

As far as young Leonardo was concerned, his home life was just fine. There was a period when Leonardo and George spent almost every weekend together. Leonardo developed an interest in museums, and for more than two years, Leonardo and his father used their Saturdays to scout out museums all over Los Angeles and Hollywood. Around the same time, Leonardo started to collect comic books. He loved going to comic-book stores with his father, who was a comic-book distributor.

Leonardo also loved to collect baseball cards, and father and son frequently attended comic-book and baseball conventions. An avid sports fan, Leonardo started collecting baseball cards as a full-time hobby; one of his favorite possessions is a rare baseball card of former Los Angeles Dodger Sandy Koufax, which his father bought for him.

"My dad has always been there for me," Leonardo says today. "I've never missed out on a so-called normal father-son relationship because I saw him anytime I wanted. Before I could drive he took me to all my auditions and helped me start my career. We've always had a lot of fun together."

Leonardo had an exciting childhood. Because Irmelin's parents still lived in Germany, she took her son on seven trips to Germany before he was ten years old. Leonardo adored his grandparents, and they loved getting to know their grandson. Irmelin had two sisters. Leonardo was the only boy in the Idenbirken family, and they loved him.

Leonardo's mother made sure these trips would be memorable for her son by teaching him German. Two of the first words he learned to say were "Oma" and "Opa," which mean "Grandma" and "Grandpa."

Leonardo loved the German countryside and spending time with his grandparents. One of his happiest memories is of going for walks in a forest called The Heart, which was near his grandparents' home. They would also take little Leonardo to the city of Düsseldorf and go shopping at the outdoor Christmas market called the Kris Kindal mart.

In a 1992 interview, Leonardo expressed his feelings about his relationship with his grandfather. "I love my grandfather because he is lots of fun to be with. I really enjoy talking with him because he always makes me laugh. He loves to joke around with me, and he cracks me up."

Because he spent so much time traveling as a child, Leonardo now loves jetting around the world. As an actor, he has done location shoots in Canada and Mexico, but he has yet to visit

Italy. Since Leonardo is one quarter Italian (his father is half German and half Italian), he longs to visit that beautiful country, especially the island of Capri. "DiCaprio" means "from Capri" in Italian. Leonardo also has relatives in Italy he has never met. Leonardo thinks it would be an incredible adventure to track down his Italian relatives someday.

Life with young Leonardo was always exciting for Irmelin, who says the young actor has always been very determined. "He started speaking when he was quite young, and once he began he just kept on going," she says with a laugh. "He was, and still is, a boy who communicates very well." Irmelin also remembers when Leonardo started to walk. "He was just nine months old when he took his first steps. But once he discovered walking he did not give up."

According to his mother, young Leonardo's favorite occupation was taking a bath. "Bath time was very exciting for him," she remembers. "It was like a big party. Leonardo would take all his action-figure toys in the tub with him, and all his animal and dinosaur toys had to be lined up around the sides. Dinosaurs have always fascinated Leo. In fact, by the time he was two or three years old, he already knew all the names of the different ones."

Leonardo grew up without brothers or sisters, but he didn't mind. He was the kind of kid who liked being the center of attention. Because his mother baby-sat for the neighborhood children, there were always other kids his age in the house.

Leonardo's mother worked a few jobs to keep food on their table. For a time, Leonardo and Irmelin lived in a run-down section of Hollywood. "We were in the poorhouse," he says. "I would walk to the playground and see a guy open up his trench coat with a thousand syringes. I lived in the ghettos of Hollywood. Right near the old Hollywood Billiards. My mom thought Hollywood was the place where all the great stuff was going on. Meanwhile it was the most disgusting place to be."

At a young age, Leonardo wanted to escape his modest beginnings. He knew there had to be a way out, and he meant to discover it. Ironically, the way out would be revealed through his stepbrother, Adam Starr. Leonardo's father had remarried and helped to raise his second wife's son. Leonardo and Adam got along very well, although they didn't see each other as often as they would have liked to.

When Leonardo was still fairly young, Adam began a television acting career. After Adam was cast in a Golden Grahams cereal commercial, it was *Leonardo*'s life that changed. Leonardo was bitten by the showbiz bug. To Leonardo, it looked like a lot of fun, and he wanted to hear all about acting from Adam.

"I asked my dad how much Adam made from the commercial," Leonardo remembers. "He said, 'About fifty thousand dollars.' Fifty thousand dollars! It just kept going through my head: *My brother has fifty thousand dollars!* That was my driving force. I remember for, like, five years thinking my brother was better than me because he had that."

Even though Adam did a bunch of commercials and was in the TV series *Battlestar Galactica,* he eventually quit acting to join the military. But that didn't stop Leonardo from hounding his parents to get *him* started in a show business career.

Leonardo was hyper, and acting provided an outlet for his energies. He kept his elementary school entertained with impersonations of famous people on the playground.

Leonardo wasn't particularly popular in school, but when he did his impressions, everyone laughed. "What I would do in order to be popular was, I would put myself on the line and joke around and be wacky and funny, and I was always known as the crazy little kid," he says. "I did impressions of everyone. Then I realized that that's not what I want to do. I don't want to be a comedian to please other people."

What he wanted to do, at the ripe old age of twelve, was go into show business full-time. Because the young attention-getter enjoyed performing so much, his parents made appointments with some agents. But getting signed proved to be a tougher project than young Leonardo had bargained for.

Some agents turned him down because they didn't like his haircut. One agent suggested that he change his name to Lenny Williams because it didn't sound as ethnic as Leonardo DiCaprio. But Leonardo would have nothing to do with that idea. If there's one thing Leonardo is proud of, it's his name.

He has made it quite clear that he hates being called anything but Leonardo. "Don't call me Leonard," he demanded in one interview. "I can't *stand* that." He is, however, affectionately called Leo by his close friends and family.

These early problems with finding an agent might have discouraged another budding young actor. But not Leonardo. He wanted to act, and his parents were doing their best to find out how to get him started.

Finally a friend of his mother's who worked for a talent agent suggested that Leonardo sign up with that agency. He did.

Now came the long and arduous job of going on countless auditions—and waiting. No one knew whether or not Leonardo would ever win any kind of role. But that never seemed to bother the future star. He was ready to put himself on the line, to read for casting directors and wait for callbacks. He never took a formal acting lesson; his attitude about acting at that time was simple: Go to a ton of auditions and keep thinking of the cash.

Leonardo always had a feeling that someday, something great would happen to him. Something would come along to turn his world upside down and plunge him into the adventure of a lifetime. He was sure acting would be his future, but he had no way of knowing how long it would take to get started.

chapter 3

THE TV KID

Leonardo's natural ability was recognized almost immediately by casting directors. He was all of fourteen years old when he began winning roles in television commercials and on television shows. With the encouragement and support of both his parents, he realized his dream very quickly.

Before he knew it, he appeared in his first commercial, for Matchbox cars. This was followed by a string of commercials for everything from cereal to toys to bubble gum. When he wasn't helping to sell products on television, he appeared in numerous educational films, such as *Mickey's Safety Club* and *How to Deal With a Parent Who Takes Drugs*.

After gaining recognition with these minor acting jobs, Leonardo won a role as a troubled teen on an episode of the TV series *Lassie*. He then had a similar role on *The Outsiders*, a short-lived TV show based on the hit movie.

Leonardo liked the parts he was playing. He quickly gained a reputation for playing teen-gone-wrong roles, and he found them very challenging. In a 1990 interview, he said, "I haven't played a cheerful boy yet. But portraying emotionally ill characters gives me the chance to really act."

And he kept getting that chance. For a short time, he joined the cast of the daytime soap opera *Santa Barbara*, playing the demanding role of a teenage alcoholic. Soap opera acting presented Leonardo with a whole new experience. He received a new script every day that had pages of dialogue for him to memorize.

Even though he had been acting for more than a year, he wasn't prepared for the frantic pace of taping a daily soap opera. Like most of the top-rated soaps, *Santa Barbara* was one hour long, and an entire show had to be taped in one day. Actors with main story lines were expected to be on the set as many as ten hours a day—or until the director was satisfied.

Because Leonardo was fifteen years old, he was only required to work on the set half a day, but that didn't ease his workload. "I had to memorize a lot of lines for the part," he said at the time, "and sometimes I had trouble. Everyone was real patient and when I messed up it wasn't that big a deal."

Keeping up with a daily soap opera and his

schoolwork was not easy for Leonardo, but he never complained. The role was short-term, and he decided to do the best job he could. He enjoyed his experience but vowed never to do another soap. It was the most grueling work he had ever done.

After *Santa Barbara* came the biggest break of Leonardo's blossoming career to that point. He won the plum role of Garry Buckman on a new half-hour sitcom called *Parenthood*. It was the chance he had hoped for, to be seen on prime-time TV every week. For Leonardo, the series represented security. It was his first truly steady job as an actor, and since he was one of the show's stars, the money was good. He was intrigued by the process of putting together a weekly TV series and wanted to learn as much as he could.

Parenthood was based on the 1989 hit movie of the same name, which had been directed by Ron Howard and starred Steve Martin. The half-hour television spin-off centered on the trials and tribulations of contemporary family life. NBC had high hopes for the show and promptly placed it in the 8 P.M. time slot on Saturday night. It debuted on August 20, 1990.

From the start, the show was not an overwhelming success, although it did get decent reviews. It was hailed by one critic as "a series about family life complete with passion and conflict." But it struggled to find an audience.

One reason may have been the size of the cast. There were fifteen regular cast members on the show, including Leonardo. The series, though funny, became much too confusing for TV audiences to keep up with.

Leonardo's character was a shy and introverted young teenager, another emotionally troubled character for him to sink his teeth into. He described the character as "a loner. He is trying to come to terms with his parents' divorce. His father won't have anything to do with the family, so I think that's mainly what makes him so quiet. It hurts him a lot."

Leonardo has fond memories of working on *Parenthood*. He made friends with the other young actors on the show. He described the cast as "one big happy family" and enjoyed going to work every day. David Arquette, who played Leonardo's brother-in-law, was only three years older, and the two struck up a strong friendship.

One month before the show debuted, Leonardo, David, and the rest of the cast excitedly attended the NBC Hot Shots party, which was the launching pad for the network's new fall lineup. Leonardo got his first real taste of posing for photographs, something he has never felt completely comfortable with. Leonardo and David were the two standout teens on *Parenthood* and were immediately written up in teen magazines.

Leonardo was touted as a "hot new idol," and in late 1990, for just five months, his face appeared in all the teen magazines. He enjoyed the exposure and said at the time that his mother was very excited to see her son in magazines. She immediately took on the job of handling all Leonardo's publicity, often contacting editors herself to see if they were interested in doing stories on him.

Leonardo's parents both kept a watchful eye on their son to make sure all the attention wasn't going to his head. Both Irmelin and George were concerned that, because he was so young, his success might change Leonardo. They soon realized that they didn't have to worry. While Leonardo enjoyed the attention he was receiving, nothing was going to change him.

George and Irmelin took turns spending time with Leonardo on the set of the show, to make sure he wasn't being taken advantage of. They helped him keep up with his schoolwork and memorize his lines.

Besides working on the show, Leonardo was also required to keep up with his schoolwork. He studied with a tutor on the set. Somehow he found time for everything:

posing for photos, studying his lines, and doing his homework. He was such a determined young man that nothing seemed too much for him to handle.

Both acting and his education meant a great deal to Leonardo. He was a straight-A student and worked to keep his grades up. Even though he enjoyed going to school, he believed that being privately tutored and studying by himself was the best way to learn. If he had any problem with his schoolwork, he would simply talk to his tutor and they would work it out.

Child actors are required by law to have a total of three hours of tutoring a day. Leonardo was working twice as hard to keep up with his schoolwork and his acting jobs. He usually made up any hours he lost during taping by studying at night or on weekends.

For most teenagers, going to school takes up the biggest part of their time. Concentrating on school and working on a TV show at the same time would be nearly impossible. But Leonardo had a blast working and studying with the four other young actors on *Parenthood*.

Unfortunately, *Parenthood* never reached the audience NBC was hoping for, and it was canceled after only four months on the air. It officially went off the air December 16, 1990, leaving Leonardo without a job. He had liked being part of a TV family, going to work every day and playing the same character each week, and he missed working on the show when it was over.

Thanks to his parents' constant support, Leonardo was able to handle the disappointment of losing *Parenthood*. But he knew that now he'd have to make the rounds of auditions again, and he wasn't looking forward to it.

Irmelin told Leonardo's agent he was interested in working on another weekly TV series, and asked the agent to send him out on an audition for a recurring role, instead of another guest-starring part. After getting a taste of working on a steady basis, Leonardo wasn't a bit interested in going backward.

Determined to do something different, he accepted a role in a film titled *Critters 3*. It marked his movie debut, but Leonardo would rather not remember it. The film was the third in a series that began with the cult horror film *Critters* in 1986. The first film was a typical horror movie. In it, eight ravenous fur balls escape from another planet and head for Earth. The film, surprisingly, received excellent reviews and did good business at the box office. *Critters 2: The Main Course* was quickly rushed out, followed by a second sequel. In *Critters 3*, the critters move into an apartment building where Leonardo's character lives.

The third *Critters* installment has gone down in movie history as one of the biggest turkeys ever, and Leonardo quickly erased it from his résumé. Fortunately, he wasn't affected by the negative reviews and comments. He did know that the movie was going to be absolutely useless in advancing his career. Looking back on it, he says, "It was possibly one of the worst films of all time. I guess it was a good example to look back on and make sure it doesn't happen again."

He continued to churn out new commercials, but for the most part he went back to school and resumed a normal life. And he waited.

His mind was on doing something bigger with every new role he accepted. He saw his career as a long climb up the ladder of success, and he wanted to keep climbing.

When he heard of the audition for a new character on the popular TV series *Growing Pains*, Leonardo hoped he'd win the role. His agent sent him on the audition, knowing that Leonardo was perfect for the part of Luke Brower, a homeless boy whose character was being written into the show as a regular.

Leonardo felt nervous but was confident

after his audition. He thought he'd done a good job and had a decent chance of getting the part. He was in the running but still had to wait for the producers' final decision. Then came the call. They wanted to see him again. It was a good sign.

Leonardo won the role of Luke Brower on *Growing Pains*, and this simple supporting character part became his ticket to the top.

chapter 4

GROWING PAINS

Growing Pains was in its last season when Leonardo DiCaprio joined the show. He was cast to add some spice to the series and get it back into the teen magazines. *Growing Pains* had launched the career of former teen idol Kirk Cameron, who played mischievous Mike Seaver on the show. It had been one of the most successful family shows of the late 1980s, and the reason why was Kirk Cameron, who pulled in a huge teenage audience.

The series hit the airwaves on September 24, 1985, on ABC, and was advertised as a new half-hour family sitcom. Alan Thicke played psychiatrist Jason Seaver, who shifted his practice to his Long Island home so that he could spend more time with his family. Joanna Kerns played his wife, Maggie, who was returning to work as a newspaper reporter; Kirk was their oldest son; Tracey Gold played their daughter,

Carol, and Jeremy Miller played their youngest son, Ben.

Over its long run, a host of new characters was added to the show. When actor Bill Kirchenbauer was introduced as Coach Lubbock, the producers decided to spin his character off into his own series called *Just the Ten of Us*, which debuted in 1988 and lasted until 1990. The producers of *Growing Pains* also decided to give Carol a new baby daughter, Chrissy, who was eventually played by child actress Ashley Johnson in the 1990 season. And, in spring 1990, Chelsea Noble joined the cast as Mike's girlfriend, Kate McDonnell. Off the set, Chelsea and Kirk were married, and both later starred on his new TV series, *Kirk*.

By the 1991–92 season, *Growing Pains* was suffering from sagging ratings. The producers were trying to find a way to breathe new life into the long-running series. Leonardo DiCaprio was their shining hope. He was cast as Luke Brower, a homeless teen who is eventually adopted by the Seaver family.

Once again, Leonardo was playing a teenager in trouble. He was thrilled when he got the news that the part was his. "I was with my mom and dad and my best friend, Toby, when my agent called," he told the teen magazine *Dream Guys*. "All of us started jumping up and down. Then I went shopping and bought a pair of eighty-dollar shoes to celebrate."

The role of Luke gave Leonardo the opportunity to expand his acting skills. It was the first time he had to cry on camera, and it was hard for him. He told *Dream Guys*, "I wasn't sure how I was going to be able to do it. But luckily the tears came when I needed them."

Leonardo analyzed his *Growing Pains* character by saying, "I liked the fact that he was homeless, yet it didn't really affect him. He tried to cover it up, but his circumstances never affected him too much. He's a nice, charming guy who knows how to weasel his way out of things."

At the time, Leonardo even addressed the issue of being homeless in an interview. "A street person isn't necessarily a bum or a depressed character," he explained. "Luke gives people a more realistic image of someone in his position—he is witty, smart, and has a good sense of humor, just like anyone else!"

Being part of a show like *Growing Pains* was a terrific experience for Leonardo. He got along great with Kirk Cameron and Jeremy Miller. Leonardo was, by this time, a full-fledged teen idol. His face graced the covers of every teen magazine on the stands. As the hot new kid on the *Growing Pains* block, he might have caused jealousy on the set. After all, Leonardo was now the one getting all the attention and exposure.

But it didn't seem to bother the others. There appeared to be a solid relationship between Leonardo and the show's other stars right from the start. Immediately seeing his potential as an actor, Tracey Gold told one reporter, "He's a great actor who will definitely go into great movies."

Kirk believed that Leonardo was doing a professional job of accepting his newfound fame. "He's coping very well. We've had long talks about it," Kirk said in an interview. "One day we walked outside the studio, and some fans came up to us. We signed autographs and kept walking. He's done very well, and he's being bombarded. I told him to have fun with it. I was always very grateful to the fans, and so is he. He's getting a lot of fan mail and is trying his best to answer it all."

As for the interaction between Kirk's character and his, Leonardo explained it by saying, "Mike is the only character on the show that Luke will let his hair down with, take a problem to, open himself up to."

The *Growing Pains* set was loads of fun for Leonardo. Kirk Cameron and Jeremy Miller loved playing practical jokes on each other. Leonardo was in the middle of one of their pranks. They told him they were going to hit each other with a water balloon. Instead, they aimed it at Leonardo and drenched him. He had never worked on a set where the actors found a way to release tension, have a good time, and still get their job done.

Leonardo considered the *Growing Pains* cast a second family. But the family didn't stay together long enough. By the middle of the seventh season, there were rumors that the show would not be coming back for an eighth year.

Growing Pains had been a terrific training ground. The show probably helped Leonardo more than anything else in his work so far. He regarded the role of Luke Brower as a springboard into his future career. Because of his popularity, there was talk that the producers would spin off Leonardo's character into his own series, but that never panned out.

The rumors of the show's cancellation continued, and Leonardo started thinking ahead. During a hiatus from *Growing Pains*, he nabbed a small role in the controversial 1992 film *Poison Ivy*, which starred Drew Barrymore. The film is about Ivy, who is taken in by a wealthy family and sets out to make the family her own. The family was played by Tom Skerritt, Cheryl Ladd, and Sara Gilbert.

The character Leonardo played in *Poison Ivy*

had no name. He was simply called Guy #1, and he had only a few lines. But that didn't matter because Leonardo loved being on the movie set. He had met Sara Gilbert, one of the stars of the hit TV series *Roseanne*, when he made a guest appearance on that show. They had become instant friends, and Leonardo was happy to get the chance to work with her again.

When *Growing Pains* officially ended its run in 1992, Leonardo knew he was finished with TV forever. He'd gone as far as he could go on television. It was time to move on. And he had already gotten a taste of what he wanted to do. His first step in a new direction was to concentrate on movies.

As it turned out, Leonardo was excused from the last four episodes of *Growing Pains* because he had already won the starring role in a new film opposite veteran actors Robert De Niro and Ellen Barkin. The opportunity would change this boy's life forever.

chapter 5

MOVING INTO MOVIES

Leonardo and his mother were vacationing in Germany when they got the news that he would be playing Tobias Wolff in the 1993 big-screen adaptation of the best-selling book *This Boy's Life*. He was so happy to win the role that he punched a hole in the ceiling!

Up to this point in his career, Leonardo had been regarded by some directors as simply a TV kid trying to break into film. There was nothing to prompt the director to give Leonardo the role in *This Boy's Life*. Nothing, that is, except his powerful audition.

When Leonardo read for the role, director Michael Caton-Jones was blown away. "It was simple. I knew he was it," Caton-Jones says. "When someone reads for you that early, you don't believe it. So we tried loads and loads of young actors, but we came right back to Leonardo."

Leonardo would eventually beat out four

hundred actors for the part. After they had met Leonardo, the filmmakers conducted a four-month casting search that encompassed Los Angeles, New York, Florida, Chicago, Seattle, Toronto, and Vancouver, looking for the perfect young actor. But no one was as good as Leonardo had been. Director Caton-Jones and producer Art Linson were in complete agreement: Leonardo DiCaprio was the *only* actor who could play the part.

It was a demanding role, but Leonardo was ready for it. For the first time, the weight of a movie rested entirely on his shoulders. He was in nearly every scene; his character was the focus of the plot.

Based on novelist Tobias Wolff's superb memoir, *This Boy's Life* is set in 1957 and tells the story of young Toby (Leonardo), who is traveling across the country with his recently divorced mother, Caroline (Ellen Barkin). Caroline's ex-husband is back east with her other son, who is attending Princeton University and living the life Toby dreams of.

Toby and Caroline settle down in Washington state, where they hope to start a new life. Unfortunately, things don't go as planned. Caroline meets and marries Dwight Hansen (Robert De Niro), who moves them to the grim, remote town of Concrete, Washington. Dwight's rigid, warped sense of right and wrong forces Toby to come to grips with his own dreams as he plots his escape from a life with no future.

It was a challenge for the director to turn the memoir into a movie. Scottish director Michael Caton-Jones, whose previous films were *Memphis Belle* and *Doc Hollywood*, knew exactly how he wanted to do it.

His idea was to take the spirit of the book and use it to his advantage. "I was determined to not make it a nice, rose-tinted look back at the past," he says. He didn't worry about the plot; he concentrated on the characters, realizing that their relationships would dictate the action. Above all, Caton-Jones recognized that this film could not have a neat, happy ending.

It was very important that Leonardo hold his own in the film and not be intimidated by Ellen Barkin and Robert De Niro. Even though De Niro was an idol of his, Leonardo never let that stand in the way of his turning in an excellent performance. "It was kind of hard not to get frightened," says Leonardo. "But I liked it when he scared me. It helped me react."

"It was very overwhelming to meet Mr. De Niro," Leonardo adds. "But I tried not to think about it. I just went in and played the part. I was confident, even though I had never done anything like it before. Now I realize it was ignorant confidence."

Director Caton-Jones was thrilled with Leonardo's ability. "I have three excellent actors in this film, especially Leonardo. He is the rock that this movie is built on. If people can't relate to the character of Toby, the story becomes voyeuristic, but Leonardo makes this kid's struggle something you can connect with immediately."

Producer Art Linson said about Leonardo, "This movie is about a kid growing up and dealing with a mother he's very close to and a stepfather he's trying to get away from. Toby's situation makes for a fascinating story, but it's also a metaphor for all the teenagers who feel similar in less desperate circumstances. Leonardo makes that possible with his performance."

In the blink of an eye, Leonardo went from *Growing Pains* heartthrob to serious actor in one of the most anticipated films of the year. It meant a lot of pressure for someone as young as Leonardo, but he pulled it off. From the first day on the set of *This Boy's Life*, Leonardo was a complete pro.

He was in good company, surrounded by some of the best actors in the business. And he learned much from working with Robert De Niro and Michael Caton-Jones. The experience made Leonardo realize how much he

Leonardo during his early years on television. He was a regular on the short-lived series *Parenthood,* and he played Luke Brower during the final season of *Growing Pains* before breaking into movies. (Copyright © 1990 by Janet Gough/Celebrity Photo)

Leonardo starred opposite Robert De Niro in *This Boy's Life.* "It was kind of hard not to get frightened," Leonardo says. "But I liked it when he scared me. It helped me react." (Copyright © 1993 by Odyssey/Shooting Star)

Young Leonardo as Tobias Wolff in *This Boy's Life*. He beat out four hundred actors for the intensely demanding role. (Copyright © 1993 by Odyssey/Shooting Star)

Leonardo with fellow actor and friend Stephen Dorff. They were both up for the role of the reporter in *Interview With the Vampire*. (Copyright © 1993 by Scott Downie/ Celebrity Photo)

Leonardo and his mother, Irmelin, arrive at the 1994 Golden Globe Awards. Leonardo received both Golden Globe and Academy Award nominations for his touching portrayal of Arnie in *What's Eating Gilbert Grape*. (Copyright © 1994 by Scott Downie/Celebrity Photo)

Leonardo in the film *The Basketball Diaries*. "I don't care about being a star," says Leonardo. "I'm concerned about being an *actor*." (Copyright © 1995 by World Films, Inc./ Shooting Star)

Leonardo and Mark Wahlberg became friends on the set of *The Basketball Diaries.* During shooting, the two actors were often spotted at New York's downtown clubs. (Copyright © 1995 by Craig Skinner/Celebrity Photo)

The cast of *The Quick and the Dead* (from left): Leonardo, Gene Hackman, Sharon Stone, and Russell Crowe. Sharon Stone gave up part of her salary so that Leonardo could join the cast. (Copyright © 1995 by TriStar Pictures/ Shooting Star)

"I'm not the sort of person who tries to be cool or trendy," says Leonardo. "I'm definitely an individual." (Copyright © 1995 by TriStar Pictures/ Shooting Star)

Working with Gene Hackman taught Leonardo a great deal about the craft of acting. (Copyright © 1995 by TriStar Pictures/ Shooting Star)

Leonardo hasn't let fame affect him. "I *insist* on keeping a level head," he says. "I really think I'm pretty well balanced being in the position I'm in." (Copyright © 1996 by Connie Ives/Hot Shot Photos)

"Leonardo is brilliant," says Claire Danes, his costar in *William Shakespeare's Romeo & Juliet*. "He's one of the most interesting people I've ever met and he is a very open, honest, and true actor." (Copyright © 1996 by Bob Ives/Hot Shot Photos)

Leonardo escorted girlfriend Kristine Zang to the premiere of *William Shakespeare's Romeo & Juliet*. (Copyright © 1996 by Lisa O'Connor/Celebrity Photo)

The fateful meeting of the star-crossed lovers in *William Shakespeare's Romeo & Juliet*. "Our version is a little more hard-core and a lot cooler," says Leonardo. (Copyright © 1996 by 20th Century Fox/Shooting Star)

Baz Luhrmann, director of *William Shakespeare's Romeo & Juliet,* says of Leonardo and Claire Danes, "Their onscreen chemistry was instant—very, very strong." (Copyright © 1996 by 20th Century Fox/Shooting Star)

Leonardo would love to take a year off from acting and travel. "I want to experience everything that is going on in the United States and overseas," he says. (Copyright © 1996 by Yoram Kahana/Shooting Star)

loved what he was doing and how much he wanted to continue acting on the silver screen.

He turned in a magnificent performance. By people unfamiliar with his TV work, Leonardo was being called Michael Caton-Jones's new discovery. Leonardo played the role in *This Boy's Life* the way he thought it should be played. The result was a portrayal mixing the innocence of adolescence with an uncontrollable anger.

How did Leonardo play the intense role of teenage Tobias Wolff so perfectly? He explains that he *became* the character. He got so involved in Toby's life story that by the end of the film, he felt emotionally drained.

"This role was different than any other I had played," he says. "This was something that was true, that actually happened to this guy. When you're in the moment of a powerful story like that, you just can't help but feel emotionally disrupted."

Principal photography on *This Boy's Life* took place on location in Vancouver. In the hills above the city, the crew built Dwight Hansen's house, where most of the film would be shot.

It was the first time Leonardo had gone on location with a film. "I loved Vancouver," he says. "Unfortunately, I worked so many hours on the film, I wasn't able to see as much of the city as I wanted to."

Leonardo also traveled to Moab and Salt Lake City, Utah, as well as Concrete, Washington, where the real Tobias Wolff had attended high school. The company rolled into the small Cascade Mountain town, a hundred miles northeast of Seattle, for ten days of filming. Hundreds of people from the town were employed as extras. Carpenters and painters returned the main street of Concrete to the way it had looked in the 1950s.

At this time, the real Tobias Wolff and his mother returned to Concrete for the first time in thirty years. Leonardo got the chance to meet the man he was playing onscreen. Leonardo asked him questions about the book and his life, but not too many. Leonardo wanted to keep some distance and play the part his way.

The reviews for *This Boy's Life* were as exceptional as the film itself. *People* magazine called it "a simply told, deeply felt story about growing up in a small town in the Fifties. Leonardo DiCaprio, in his first major movie role, carries the film with impressive ease, letting you see the hurt beneath this kid's affected toughness."

Movieline magazine singled out Leonardo's performance by saying, "DiCaprio's childlike face can slip from innocence to insolence in a moment. The natural sophistication of his acting anchors a film that is all about unspoken feelings and unnameable desires."

The New Yorker hailed the film as "absorbing" and said "DiCaprio is sensational!" Film critics Gene Siskel and Roger Ebert gave the film "two thumbs up," with Siskel saying Leonardo was "simply terrific."

Movie audiences also responded enthusiastically to "newcomer" Leonardo DiCaprio. With his gripping portrayal of Tobias Wolff, he was now clearly positioned to be one of Hollywood's hot new stars. His standout performance earned him the New Generation Award from the Los Angeles Film Critics Association.

Leonardo's career was suddenly on a roll, and his next offer was just around the corner.

chapter 6

WHAT'S EATING
GILBERT GRAPE

While still wrapping *This Boy's Life*, Leonardo already had another project in the works, one that would be the most exciting of his career. He was cast as Arnie Grape in the offbeat 1993 comedy-drama *What's Eating Gilbert Grape.* Leonardo's performance as Arnie will likely be remembered as one of the best of his career.

The part is indeed the most ambitious one Leonardo had ever played. The director, Swedish-born Lasse Hallström (*My Life as a Dog, Once Around,*) says he chose Leonardo because he liked the distance in his eyes. But the director did take some convincing. Hallström admits that he was at first afraid Leonardo's good looks would distract moviegoers from Arnie's mental disabilities. But Leonardo convinced him he was right for the part.

The movie is about young Gilbert Grape (Johnny Depp), the man of the Grape household. He lives in a ramshackle farmhouse in

Endora, Iowa, with his five-hundred-pound mother (Darlene Cates), his brother, Arnie (Leonardo), and his two sisters, Amy (Laura Harrington) and Ellen (Mary Kate Schellhardt). Gilbert works as a clerk at the Lamson Grocery Store and fantasizes about leaving Endora, where he feels trapped.

He is in charge of taking care of his mother, who hasn't left the house in seven years, and his brother (played by Leonardo), who insists on climbing the town water tower, much to the annoyance of the local police. Gilbert's best buddies are Bobby (Crispin Glover), the undertaker's son, who drives a hearse around town to promote business, and Tucker (John C. Reilly), who sees a soon-to-be-opened Burger Barn as a rare job opportunity.

When a young woman named Becky (Juliette Lewis) travels through town, Gilbert finds himself attracted to this outsider, who also notices him. Her arrival becomes the first in a series of surprising events in the life of Gilbert Grape.

To play the poignantly troubled brother, Arnie, Leonardo decided to "get rid of everything I would normally do."

In researching his character, Leonardo watched videos of mentally challenged young people and met many others. He also traveled with Hallström to Texas and spent a few days at a home for mentally disabled teenagers.

"People have these expectations that retarded children are really crazy and 'out there,'" says Leonardo. "But it's refreshing to see them. Everything is new to them.

"When I first started, I was trying to process all of the information—the various twitches, certain ways of moving, facial expressions," he continues. "I realized there were many different ways to do this role, thousands of different things I could do."

Leonardo met a young autistic man, whom he eventually used as his model for the role. "I took a lot of his mannerisms and made them more like my own," says Leonardo. "I developed the character even more by adding mannerisms of some of the other people I had met."

Leonardo was concerned about his final performance and worried about how he would look onscreen as Arnie. His hair in the film looked as if someone had cut it by putting a bowl on his head. And he had to wear a mouthpiece to give Arnie a slightly deformed look. "I had a chili-bowl haircut. I looked so vile, but it was great," he says.

Leonardo thought his appearance was right on target, and that it helped add realism and intensity to his portrayal.

"I was surprised Arnie wasn't overbearingly obnoxious," Leonardo comments. "I didn't think he was going to be as charming as he was."

For the role of Gilbert Grape, Hallström selected Johnny Depp, the actor who gained fame playing quirky characters in movies like *Edward Scissorhands*, *Cry-Baby*, *Benny & Joon*, and *Ed Wood*.

Also joining the cast were Juliette Lewis (*Cape Fear*, *Kalifornia*) as Becky, the object of Gilbert's affections, and, as Momma, Darlene Cates, whom Leonardo adored. Cates caught the director's attention when he saw her on an episode of the Sally Jessy Raphaël talk show about overweight women who hadn't left their homes in several years. Leonardo says Darlene "was the sweetest woman that I ever met in my entire life. I still talk to her every once in a while."

Leonardo also got along well with Johnny Depp. Like Leonardo, Johnny got his start on television, in the hit series *21 Jump Street*. He had tasted fame quickly and became a teen idol at a young age. Like Leonardo, he tried— successfully—to play more serious roles.

The onscreen chemistry these two actors shared spilled over into an an offscreen camaraderie. To release the tensions of playing their serious roles, Leonardo and Johnny would often engage in some good old-fashioned fun.

"Johnny loved to see my facial expressions when I was disgusted by the smell of something," says Leonardo, laughing. "Whenever there was something gross around, he'd give it to me to smell, and I would do this gagging thing."

Johnny teased Leonardo until he couldn't take it anymore. Johnny would bring in things like rotten eggs and pickled sausage, until Leonardo started charging him money for making faces. "I made about five hundred dollars," Leonardo says.

Leonardo feels sure he wouldn't have been able to portray Arnie so perfectly if he hadn't had Johnny to play the character against. "Johnny was *extremely* like Gilbert," Leonardo says. "But it wasn't something Johnny was trying to do. It naturally came out of him. I never quite understood what he was going through, because it wasn't some big emotional drama that was happening every day on the set—but subtle things I'd see in him would make me question what was going on. There's an element of Johnny that's extremely nice and extremely cool, but at the same time, he's hard to figure out. That's what makes him interesting."

Alan C. Blomquist, the film's executive producer, regards Leonardo's Arnie as a balance to Johnny Depp's Gilbert. "Leonardo gives Arnie this childlike quality," says Blom-quist, "playing him very free and open and honest. He's a great counterpart to Johnny, whose character is so solemn and serious about life."

When the reviews for *What's Eating Gilbert Grape* rolled in, everyone praised Leonardo's work. One critic wrote, "As Arnie, DiCaprio is nothing short of extraordinary. Though the film verges on worship of the retarded— Arnie is the most loving character in the film—he is also weird, embarrassing, and in-furiating, and DiCaprio's body language is extremely accurate."

Another critic said, "What held *Gilbert Grape* together was DiCaprio's amazing, instinctive performance."

Entertainment Weekly announced, "Leo-nardo DiCaprio, the vibrant young star of *This Boy's Life*, gives an audacious and technically amazing performance as Arnie. This is one boy who commands your attention."

Movieline magazine said, "DiCaprio, who also won acclaim in last year's *This Boy's Life*, does the best retarded character I've ever seen in a movie. He does what Dustin Hoffman *thought* he was doing in *Rain Man*."

Leonardo handed in such an authentic per-formance, it not only stunned the filmmakers, critics, and moviegoers, but it also made the Academy Award voters sit up and take notice. When the Academy Award nominations were read in early 1994, Leonardo DiCaprio was honored with a well-deserved Best Supporting Actor nomination. He also received the Los Angeles Film Critics Association New Generation Award again, as well as a National Board of Review Award. But it was the Oscar nomination that made him the most nervous. It was an amazing moment for Leonardo, one of happiness and wrenching fear.

"I was dreading winning," he says. "And there were some people who were saying, 'Hey, you might have a chance.' And I was saying, 'No, no, I'm not going to win.' I was convincing myself. I didn't even plan a speech. If it did happen, I just would've thanked everyone and got off the stage. You don't want to sound too preachy."

The Academy Awards were difficult for Leonardo. He's always had a problem with speaking in front of big audiences. "I worried that I would slip up or do something horrible," he says. "Or cry, something that's embarrassing. I put that pressure on myself."

Then came the big night. He arrived at the ceremonies with his mother, father, and stepmother. "I was so nervous my palms started to sweat, and I just started to twitch," he says. "When I got to the awards, people were telling me, 'You know, you have a pretty good chance of winning tonight.' And this thing started to consume me. I was shaking in my seat and putting on this posed smile, and inside I was petrified."

The show started, but that didn't calm Leonardo down. What made matters worse was that his mother got up to go to the rest room right before his category was read and couldn't get back into the auditorium. "I'm sitting there and they said, 'Okay, the nominees for Best Supporting Actor are . . . ,' and my mom wasn't there! And I knew if my mom wasn't there, it would be terrible. I saw this guard holding my mom back. She was trying to jump through a bunch of people, and they showed the first nominee and said, 'Tommy Lee Jones in *The Fugitive.*'

"I knew I had to do something. My mom *had* to be next to me. So I turned to the security guards and I mouthed, 'Let her in.' The guy looked at me, and I said, 'I'm a nominee.' I never do that kind of thing, but I figured this was really important. And my mom just scooted by and jumped in the seat and in five seconds she adjusted herself, I adjusted myself, and I was sitting there with this smile on my face like nothing had happened. Meanwhile, I'm about ready to die. When they announced Tommy Lee Jones had won, I wanted to get down on the ground and thank God. Nobody was happier for him than me, that's the truth."

Before Leonardo had done *Gilbert Grape*, he still wasn't sure where he wanted to go as an actor. He had read for a variety of roles in a variety of movies. At the time, he felt all movies were basically the same. He used to look at it this way: If he could win *any* role at all, that was great. At least he was doing what he loved.

"I didn't know what type of movies I wanted to do. I just felt like doing a movie is doing a movie. I get money and fame, and that's great, and I can act and have fun. I was up for a movie called *Hocus Pocus* with Bette Midler. I knew it was awful, but it was like, 'Okay, they're offering me more and more money. Isn't that what you do? You do movies and you get more and more money.'

"But something inside of me kept saying, 'Don't do this movie.' And everyone around me was saying, 'Leonardo, how could you not take a movie?' I said to myself, 'Okay, I'll audition for this other one, *Gilbert Grape*. If I don't get that, I'll do *Hocus Pocus*.'

"I found myself trying so hard, investing so

much time and energy in *Gilbert Grape*. I worked so hard at it and I finally got it, and it was such a weight off my shoulders."

What came out of Leonardo's *Gilbert Grape* experience was the understanding that he never wanted to do films he didn't believe in. He regards playing Arnie as "the most fun I've ever had."

In an interview after the film had been released, Leonardo explained where he wanted to go next with his career. "I want to do things that are different," he said. "Not necessarily different just to be different, but something that I can get into with other actors who are quality actors and a quality director and a good script."

No one could deny that Leonardo had climbed to the top in competitive Hollywood in a very short time. Even *he* didn't know how he had been able to pull it off.

Leonardo signed with Creative Artists Agency and set out to make an entirely new image for himself. He had starred in two very important films in a little more than one year and real-ized it was worth all the hard work he had put into them. He was now very serious about his future work. "I never realized how much I really loved acting until after I did *What's Eating Gilbert Grape*," he says. "I love it when you get to create stuff, and collaborate with a director. You feel like what you're doing is not going to waste. It's in the archives. It's going to be there for years. Michael Caton-Jones, the director of *This Boy's Life*, said to me: 'Pain is temporary, film is forever.' That's my favorite quote."

Leonardo vowed to avoid doing unimportant films in the future, and to concentrate on high-quality roles. Would that be an easy task? He didn't know for sure, but he was ready for the challenge.

"I'm not saying I want to be Mr. Dark Underground Artist and only do smaller type films, but those are the only ones that have any real content," he announced in an interview.

By the end of 1993, Leonardo DiCaprio was considered a "hot property" in Hollywood. After the praise he won for *This Boy's Life* and *What's Eating Gilbert Grape*, it looked like smooth sailing for Leonardo.

But there was some heavy weather ahead. For one, he publicly announced how much he wanted to play Malloy, the interviewer in *Interview With the Vampire*, after the untimely death of River Phoenix, who had originally been cast in the role. Leonardo read for the role and was brilliant, but he was too young. David Geffen, the film's producer, decided on Christian Slater instead.

Leonardo was crushed by the news; he

really wanted to be part of that film. It was one of several disappointments he would face in the year ahead.

As he entered 1994, he would experience some highs and lows. And for the first time in life, his career would be on the line.

chapter 7

HOLLYWOOD'S TOP YOUNG GUN

After he lost the role of the reporter in *Interview With the Vampire*, Leonardo decided to take the next interesting part that came along. That happened to be the title role in a twenty-minute film called *The Foot Shooting Party*, which was executive produced by director Renny Harlin.

Harlin, best known in Hollywood as a director of action-adventure films, had carved out a successful career for himself. He had directed *Cliffhanger* with Sylvester Stallone, *Die Hard 2* with Bruce Willis, and, more recently, *The Long Kiss Goodnight*, starring his wife, Geena Davis.

Leonardo played the lead in *The Foot Shooting Party*, which is about a rock-and-roll singer in the early 1970s who must choose whether to go to Vietnam or put a bullet in his foot to avoid the draft.

The short film was a great learning experience for Leonardo. It gave him the chance to work with a director whose films he admired, and to dress up in the outrageous styles of the 1970s. In the film, Leonardo wore bell-bottoms and had hair extensions added to his fine blond locks. The film was one of the most interesting projects Leonardo worked on. It was released by Touchstone Pictures, but unfortunately most moviegoers didn't get a chance to see it.

Had Leonardo taken too much of a risk in accepting the role in *The Foot Shooting Party*? He didn't think so. In many ways, he related more to that short film than he did to his next project.

His agent informed him that Sharon Stone (*Basic Instinct, Casino*) was coproducing a new Western called *The Quick and the Dead* and wanted Leonardo for one of the lead characters. Before even reading the script, Leonardo heard the word "Western" and was sure he wasn't interested.

"It was honestly not my idea of the type of movie I wanted to do next," he says. "I really had to think it through for a long time."

Stone and the filmmakers were patient. She knew she would have to work on convincing Leonardo to join the cast. It wouldn't be easy, but Stone didn't let that stand in her way.

British writer Simon Moore (*Under Suspicion, Traffick*), who had never ventured into the American West, came up with the film's premise. Moore's script eventually landed in the hands of independent producer Allen Shapiro, who sent it to Sharon Stone. She instantly loved it and wanted to do it.

Sam Raimi, the master of comedy-horror movies such as *The Evil Dead*, *Darkman*, and *Army of Darkness*, was Stone's first and only choice for director. "If he didn't do it, I didn't want to make the movie," she says. "I think Westerns peaked with *Unforgiven*, and I wasn't interested in chasing that genre in that same classic way."

Luckily, Raimi accepted the job and attempted "to make a straightforward, fast-paced action film. Our goal is to entertain. It's a tale of the Old West, but with a female in the lead.

"This is the Old West of our fantasies," explains Raimi. "Realism was not our goal. We weren't making a documentary. Admittedly, we owe more to Sergio Leone's spaghetti Westerns of the 1960s than to the John Ford classic Westerns of the 1940s."

Next, Stone fought to get Russell Crowe signed as her love interest in the film. The studio didn't want him, but Sharon Stone did, and that was all that mattered. Crowe was signed.

The Quick and the Dead is the story of Ellen, a mysterious young woman who rides into the town of Redemption with a six-gun strapped to her hip and revenge burning in her heart. She has come to town to kill Herod (Gene Hackman), the man who murdered her father years before.

As the mayor of Redemption, Herod stages a deadly annual quick-draw tournament that lures hometown hopefuls as well as gun-slingers from all over the West. He uses it to weed out his rivals and prove he's still the fastest gun in town. His rules are simple: Anyone who signs up can challenge another contestant to a duel. Whoever is left standing walks away with the cash prize, while the other contestant faces death.

Sharon Stone says of her character, "Ellen is tough, crafty, as intelligent as any man in town. But she's paralyzed by the past and can't go on with her life until she deals with it. She thinks she can simply walk in and do what she has to do: kill the man who murdered her father. When she's faced with reality, the mission becomes enormously complicated. Finally, she has to face her own demons before she confronts Herod, the terrifying ruler of Redemption."

Stone wanted Leonardo for the role of the Kid, who is Herod's estranged son. As coproducer of the film, Stone insisted on Leonardo and fought to get him signed. "I wanted him bad, and we'd topped out financially," says Stone, who agreed to pay Leonardo's fee out of her own salary.

Leonardo had already turned down the project. He wasn't agreeing to anything the filmmakers were offering him. The producers were ready to cast another actor in the part but decided to give Leonardo one last try. "My agent called and told me, 'Look, they really want you, and this is the last day you can have the role, because they are going to hire somebody else,'" Leonardo remembers. "Everyone around me was saying, 'This is a good movie.' I had this thing about not doing big commercial movies because most of the mainstream movies are just pieces of garbage that have been done over a thousand times.

"Then I looked at *The Quick and the Dead*, and I thought, *Okay, Sharon Stone is in it, Gene Hackman is in it, and Sam Raimi is a completely innovative director. I thought, I'm not working, I could do something different and I can have fun with this movie.*" Leonardo felt that Sharon Stone really believed in the movie and in his talent. Finally the apprehensive young actor agreed to play the Kid.

With Leonardo signed on, the cast was complete and ready to begin shooting. *The*

Quick and the Dead, which takes place over a four-day period in 1878, was filmed in Mescal, Arizona, about forty miles east of Tucson. The Western street owned by Old Tucson Studios had been used for several other Western films, beginning with a 1970 Lee Marvin film called *Monte Walsh*. The same street was again used in *The Life and Times of Judge Roy Bean* (1972) with Paul Newman, and in *Tombstone* (1993) with Kurt Russell.

Leonardo loved running around the street set and getting into Western garb for his role. He was also interested in learning how to shoot a gun. Thell Reed, who has been working with movie productions as a gun coach since 1958, was hired to teach Leonardo and the cast how to hold a gun the right way and how to strap on a holster. He found Leonardo a good student. Part of his coaching included a series of martial arts–like moves, which Leonardo picked up immediately.

"I see the Kid as a good version of Billy the Kid. My character is somebody who is so completely insecure in himself that he has to put on a show to dazzle everybody, and that, to me, was very interesting," says Leonardo. "He develops this thing about being cool. He is only afraid of his father. He's cocky and confident until he gets around his father. Then he just begs for attention by trying to prove he can kill faster and better than anyone else in town. He's a sad case but a really interesting character to play."

In a climactic showdown with Herod, his father, Leonardo's character is finally put to the test. "The Kid thinks he can't die," explains Leonardo. "All he wants out of life is his father's respect. He'll go to any lengths for that recognition."

Unfortunately, he never gets it. Herod kills his son in a duel near the film's end. It was the first death scene Leonardo had played on the big screen, and he threw himself into it, delivering a tear-filled, heart-wrenching performance that brings the movie to a halt. The audience sees the Kid, who has tried to be so tough and confident throughout the picture, crumble as he lies dying. Still thinking he's the fastest young gun in town, the Kid waits for the approval and respect of his father, but he never gets it. He dies knowing his father killed him.

When *The Quick and the Dead* was released, it received mixed reviews. Most critics didn't like seeing Sharon Stone as a female gunfighter. And Gene Hackman had just played a role similar to that of Herod in Clint Eastwood's *Unforgiven*, so there was no surprise for moviegoers seeing him in another Western film.

Leonardo received the best reviews. *Entertainment Weekly* said, "Of the secondary characters, the only one who escapes sketchbook thinness is Herod's son, a precocious teen gunslinger played by Leonardo Dicaprio in a performance so guileless and cocky he's like a junior version of Jon Voight in *Midnight Cowboy*."

As for the film itself, *Entertainment Weekly* went on to say, "*The Quick and the Dead* is too light to pack the dramatic punch of a true Western. It ends up in its own amiable, slow-poke limbo."

The Quick and the Dead died at the box office. Leonardo could easily have been upset that the film wasn't a huge success, but he had no time to worry. Of the film, he said, "It was fun, and I'm glad I was part of it."

By the time *The Quick and the Dead* hit theaters in February 1995, Leonardo had already finished filming another movie. *The Basketball Diaries*, shot almost entirely on location in New York City, would bring him more recognition than he had planned on. And not all of it was positive.

chapter 8

DEVELOPING A STYLE

The Basketball Diaries intrigued Leonardo from the moment he read the script. "It was the first time where I actually read a script and I didn't want to put it down," he remembers. "It's rare when you find something raw. Writing so completely honest that after reading it, you know the person—the way they are, the way they think, what they went through and the way they lived as a human being."

The story was powerful; it made an important statement about drug abuse; and Leonardo wanted to play the lead role.

The Basketball Diaries is based on the critically acclaimed memoirs of Jim Carroll's adolescent years as a Catholic high-school basketball star, which vividly described how he and his friends spiraled downward into a frightening world of drugs and crime.

Jim Carroll's basketball diaries first appeared in *The Paris Review* in the late 1960s. In 1978, his best-selling book was published, capturing the interest of filmmakers. The book sold an estimated half million copies and turned Carroll into an overnight media star. The same year, he released his *Catholic Boys* album on the Rolling Stones' record label, also to overwhelmingly positive reviews and soaring sales.

Over the years, several production companies and studios hoped to turn *The Basketball Diaries* into a movie. Rising young stars Matt Dillon, Eric Stoltz, Johnny Depp, and River Phoenix (who died during the filming of *Interview With the Vampire*) all wanted to play Carroll. In the late 1980s, River Phoenix was so interested in *The Basketball Diaries* that he carried the book in his pocket, saying it was the only lead role he wanted to play.

Over a period of fifteen years, ten scripts were written, more than seven directors mentioned, and several film studios interested in *The Basketball Diaries*. Hollywood executives continually turned down the project, partly because of President Ronald Reagan's "war on drugs" campaign in the 1980s. With everyone "saying no to drugs," studio executives decided not to take a chance on the story. They waited until the time seemed right.

The project eventually started to move toward production in 1993, after Island Pictures producer Liz Heller teamed up with music video director Scott Kalvert.

"Scott was extremely passionate about the material, and I was about to option the book," says Heller. "I was fascinated by it because it was a film for and about today's youth."

They knew they had to find the right young actor for the lead role if the film was to be as electrifying as they hoped. After seeing Leonardo's performance in *This Boy's Life*, Heller and Kalvert asked his agent at Creative Artists Agency to send him the script. Leonardo loved it and wanted to play the role, but was leery after meeting Kalvert.

"He had done these Marky Mark videos," says Leonardo. "That was a bit of a problem. I wanted to do this movie, but I didn't want it to turn out to be some After School Special about drugs, which it might have turned out to be."

What eventually changed Leonardo's mind was that he liked Kalvert. "He seemed like a cool guy," Leonardo says. "He was willing to listen to my opinions."

With Leonardo in place as Jim, casting began for three actors to portray his friends Mickey, Pedro, and Neutron. James Madio and Patrick McGaw won the roles of Pedro and Neutron. For the role of Mickey, Kalvert suggested former rap singer and Calvin Klein underwear model Mark "Marky Mark" Wahlberg, whom Kalvert had directed in numerous award-winning music videos.

Marky Mark in a movie? Leonardo thought the idea was terrible. "Like any normal human being, I freaked out," he recalls. "I figured a singer like that was not right for the part. I told Scott, 'No, we can't audition him.' He said, 'I worked with Marky and he's a really cool guy.' And I said, 'Absolutely not. There's plenty of cool people out there, just find one of them.'"

Eventually Leonardo came to feel that he wasn't being fair to Mark Wahlberg and decided to give him a chance. "As soon as I met him, I wanted to find something wrong with him," Leonardo explains. "I thought he was going to be terrible in the movie. But he did the scene, and I couldn't help but be charmed by what he did. He brought an element of reality to it, and he brought an element of being truly street, because that's what he is. And he was the best person for the role by far."

Leonardo and Mark Wahlberg became good friends on the set of *The Basketball Diaries.* They were complete cut-ups, always joking around between takes. While shooting a scene at a luncheonette in Hoboken, New Jersey, one night, the two actors were spotted dropping candy from the roof onto passersby.

The Basketball Diaries was shot in eight weeks with a modest budget of $4 million. It was filmed almost entirely on the streets of New York, in some of the locations described in Jim Carroll's book. A large portion was shot in and around Tompkins Square Park in the East Village, not far from St. Mark's Place, where Jim Carroll first gained literary recognition.

Filming in New York City was a big deal for Leonardo. "I love New York. I want to move here," he said during the production. "You could sit at one corner all day and probably have a more fulfilling day than traveling all over L.A. and seeing all the sights."

The movie crew had a tough time filming in public places because Leonardo was becoming so well known. He attracted crowds everywhere he went. A surprising number of people, especially teenage girls, followed him around asking for autographs.

According to one crew member, whenever Leonardo walked down the street, he looked like the Pied Piper of Hamelin, with herds of teenage girls walking behind him.

Leonardo had a great time filming *The Basketball Diaries.* He enjoyed seeing the sights of the city with Marky Mark and his *Gilbert Grape* costar Juliette Lewis, who was also in *The Basketball Diaries.* Leonardo also loved working with Lorraine Bracco, who played his mother, and with Bruno Kirby.

"Lorraine is the best woman I've ever worked with. I kept messing up a scene and Lorraine was the only one who said, 'You can do it,' " says Leonardo. "And working with Bruno was a thrill because I loved him in *When Harry Met Sally. . . .*"

Leonardo also valued the opinions of Jim Carroll, who was on the set for much of the shoot and had a bit part in the film. When *The Basketball Diaries* was released in theaters, Leonardo accompanied Carroll on book signings, and both author and the actor who played him signed new copies of the book.

One of the only things that upset Leonardo was the fact that the press was following him around and writing about his partygoing habits. He admits he partied during the filming of *The Basketball Diaries*, but says the stories in the gossip columns were greatly exaggerated.

"They want to title me the Young Hollywood hotshot who all of a sudden goes rampant," he says. "They don't see me hanging out in my hotel room or doing normal things."

"Marky and I went out at night or on weekends. We had a good time at the clubs. That was all, but they wanted to escalate it into something different, which is what the tabloids are all about. At one point they said we had a fistfight with Derrick Coleman, the basketball player, and that wasn't true. Apparently, he was in the same club we were in, but I never even saw the guy. They wrote up a lot of stuff like that."

To prepare for his role as the poet and rocker hooked on heroin, Leonardo spent time with a drug counselor. Leonardo says he was completely naive when it came to showing the effects of drugs on the body.

"I knew the basics," he says. "What makes you hyper, what makes you drowsy. But I relied on a counselor to learn about the specific behavioral nuances."

When *The Basketball Diaries* was released, critics once again praised Leonardo's performance. *People* magazine wrote, "Leonardo DiCaprio proves yet again that he's the most promising actor around. DiCaprio's performance is flawless. The real pleasure is observing how naturally he carries himself in front of the camera."

But glowing notices for Leonardo did not help save *The Basketball Diaries.* Maybe the subject matter was still too dark for moviegoers. The movie didn't do as well as the filmmakers had expected.

After all the hard work Leonardo had put

into *The Basketball Diaries*, it had only a short life in theaters. Leonardo was at a crossroads in his career. He was undecided about what he should do next.

Warner Brothers was planning a big-budget movie about the life of James Dean, and Leonardo was chosen to play Dean. He had a lot of reservations about portraying the renowned actor, who died in 1955 after a brief but brilliant career. "You have to think twice about this kind of role," Leonardo said in an interview. "There are good things and bad things about it. On one side it's a great character. On the other side, I could do nothing but duplicate Dean. There's no way to duplicate him exactly. Nobody can do that, it's impossible. There is pressure if you do James Dean because people are going to be critical of you."

Leonardo remained in negotiations for the James Dean movie until he was offered the role of the nineteenth-century French poet Arthur Rimbaud. He had two scripts in his hand; both were biographies of legendary figures, and Leonardo didn't know which one to take.

He decided to ask Jim Carroll which role he should choose. "I held up two scripts and said, 'Hey, Jim, James Dean or Arthur Rimbaud?' He said, 'Man, you're crazy. Arthur Rimbaud is the coolest!' That helped me decide!"

So Leonardo next began work on *Total Eclipse*, playing another emotionally intense person. A few people close to Leonardo discouraged him from making that choice because they were afraid the film's subject matter might tarnish his image. But Leonardo didn't listen. Before he knew it, he was on a plane heading for France, where the film was shot.

Total Eclipse is the fact-based story of Arthur Rimbaud, a rebellious teenage poet in nineteenth-century France who lived life to the extreme and died at thirty-seven years old. The film focuses on Rimbaud's tormented relationship with the poet Paul Verlaine (David Thewlis).

Leonardo describes this role as "one of the most important of my career and one of the best roles to play for a young actor. Rimbaud wanted to change the world from one day to the next. He was someone courageous, who didn't worry about the consequences of his actions. I live my life thinking of the consequences. Shooting this film, I learned not to worry about what others think of what I am doing. It has definitely changed me."

Rimbaud was homosexual, and that was the part of the film most critics focused on when reviewing *Total Eclipse*. As for Leonardo, he didn't have a problem with doing a film that portrayed a relationship between two men.

"That's just acting, but as far as the kissing stuff, that was a little hard for me," he admits.

As always, Leonardo's performance was singled out as phenomenal. But the movie was not a hit with audiences.

What had gone wrong? *Total Eclipse* seemed to be the biggest risk Leonardo had taken in his career. "People hated this movie," he says. "I wanted to do the part because Rimbaud was a genius. I think the only people who liked *Total Eclipse* were people who like Rimbaud. But then, a lot of people who liked Rimbaud hated it too. I don't know what to say about *Total Eclipse.* We filmed it in France, and over there Rimbaud is like James Dean. But in the United States people really don't know who he is. I think maybe the film didn't explain enough."

Leonardo had starred in two films that had done poorly at the box office. Suddenly the hot new rising star was falling. As easygoing as ever, Leonardo didn't let it bother him.

He believed he had done the right thing by accepting these two roles. They gave him a chance to develop his style, stretch his acting talents, and prove he could tackle any part with ease. The kid who had begun his career in television commercials had proved he was willing to take chances and test his limits as an actor. Leonardo likes to keep challenging himself; never, for one minute, did he regret doing *The Basketball Diaries* and *Total Eclipse.*

"I'm really glad I did those two movies. I'm proud of my work in them," he says. "In five years nobody will remember any of the bad reviews, and my work in them will be seen as part of all my work. I'm not worried about that."

He *was* worried about what he should do next but decided not to think about it. After working on so many films in a row, he was exhausted. He needed some time to get away from acting. He needed time to go home, see his friends and his family, and just relax.

He knew his next choice had to be something special, and he decided he would wait for it if he had to. But he didn't need to wait long.

In less than one year, Leonardo DiCaprio bounced back in a big way, playing a modern-day Romeo in the sizzling *William Shakespeare's Romeo & Juliet.*

chapter 9

ROCK-AND-ROLL ROMEO

Leonardo's first reaction to the idea of a new version of William Shakespeare's *Romeo and Juliet* was "Why do *Romeo and Juliet* again? It has been done so many times, and so many people loved the 1968 Franco Zeffirelli film."

That was before Australian director Baz Luhrmann contacted Leonardo with a reworking of the classic story in a modern setting. Luhrmann, who began his career as an actor, had become an overnight sensation when the first film he directed premiered at the 1992 Cannes Film Festival. The critically hailed *Strictly Ballroom* not only became a box office hit, but also won a truckload of awards, including eight Australian Film Institute Awards, three British Academy Awards, and a Golden Globe nomination.

Luhrmann knew he had to do something spectacular for an encore, so he took a few years off and decided to make a new *Romeo and Juliet.* For his second feature, he wanted to film a fast-paced, sexy, fresh version of the classic love story. The more Luhrmann worked on the idea, the more it excited him. He started to comb through the citizens of Young Hollywood for the perfect actors to play the star-crossed lovers.

Luhrmann had seen Leonardo's photograph in a magazine and thought he'd make a perfect Romeo. He invited Leonardo to Australia to participate in several workshops and to discuss the project with him.

"The deal I made with Leo was, 'Look, don't agree to do it,'" Luhrmann remembers. "'But don't decline it yet, either. Come to Australia, work with me for a week at this little rehearsal space I've got in a theater on the harbor, and see how you like it.'"

What had Baz Luhrmann seen in Leonardo that convinced him Leonardo was perfect for a Romeo of the 1990s? Luhrmann needed to cast an actor who was excellent onscreen, who could display vital energy and emotion, and—to get the film financed—who was a bankable box office star. The only actor who measured up was Leonardo DiCaprio.

But Leonardo was not interested. It was only after Luhrmann had explained his vision that Leonardo decided to sign on to play Romeo. To get financing for the movie, Leonardo agreed to film a test scene for Luhrmann, which the director sent to 20th Century Fox studios. It was Leonardo's scene and his star status that convinced the studio to give the Australian director a budget for the movie.

The thing that most interested Leonardo about Luhrmann's vision was the setting of the film in what he calls a "created world," a collage of modern and classic images drawn from folklore, pop culture, the theater, and technology. In Luhrmann's *Romeo & Juliet*, swords are replaced by guns, and Shakespeare's setting of Verona, Italy, becomes Verona Beach, U.S.A.

Leonardo says, "What Baz has done is reinvent [the play], and in the process, he's discovered new ways of treating the play and the characters. The created world really helped me, as an actor. It heightened everything, which made it more dangerous, more interesting and more liberating. It gave me more freedom to try different things with the character and the scenes, because we were not held down by traditional rules."

With Leonardo cast as Romeo, Luhrmann began a "worldwide search" for Juliet. Every young actress in Hollywood, including Alicia Silverstone and Natalie Portman, auditioned for the role. Leonardo was right there, playing the same scene with every actress trying out. It was a tiring part of his job, especially since Luhrmann couldn't seem to find an actress good enough to be cast in the role.

When Claire Danes came in, both Leonardo and Luhrmann knew they had found Juliet. "She was strong with Leonardo," says Luhrmann.

Leonardo also praised Claire's audition. "She was the only one who came right up and said the lines directly to me," he says. "It was a little shocking, but it impressed me because most of the other girls auditioning looked off into the sky. Claire was right there, in front of my face, saying every line with power."

Actually, it was no surprise that Claire Danes won the role. She is, after all, the best young actress to emerge in Hollywood in a long time. She first gained attention as Angela on the critically acclaimed TV series *My So-Called Life*. The show didn't last long, but Claire's performance was recognized with an Emmy nomination and a Golden Globe Award for Best Actress in a television drama.

Claire quickly moved into films, making her feature debut as Beth in the 1994 version of *Little Women* with Winona Ryder. She followed that role with the films *How to Make an American Quilt, Home for the Holidays,* and *To Gillian on Her 37th Birthday.*

Claire was excited to learn she would be

playing Juliet, saying the role "is remarkable because she [Juliet] is determined and mature, but at the same time, she has an innocence to her, a youth and a freshness. She is very thoughtful, smart and passionate. She is an incredibly modern character who makes her own decisions and takes fate into her own hands."

The flame that smoldered between Leonardo and Claire was obvious from the first day they worked together. John Leguizamo, who plays the villainous Tybalt in the film, says of his two costars, "I think they had crushes on each other but they kept it very professional. Nothing was ever done. And that's great, because when you consummate an attraction you totally defuse the tension on the screen."

Luhrmann was thrilled with the electricity between Leonardo and Claire. He says, "One thing that I have absolutely no doubt about in this film is their onscreen chemistry. It's the sort of thing that's so defined. You can have two fantastic actors and still, the moment you see them onscreen, it's either there or it's not. They absolutely had it. And as it turned out, Leonardo and Claire were like brother and sister on the set."

There was no denying that they got along, but flare-ups did occur. They spent so much time together that there was some tension between them.

"There were arguments. They went through some very difficult times emotionally on the set. There were definitely times when all three of us sniped at each other," Luhrmann admits. "Sometimes Leo and Claire were like two kids on holiday and sometimes it was like you were dragging your children through a desert and they were starving and suffering. But because they were so young and in the middle of such extraordinary events, I think they came to rely on each other, which was a great thing to behold."

Before the filming of *William Shakespeare's Romeo & Juliet*, Luhrmann had Leonardo and Claire rehearse extensively. He wanted to be sure they understood the characters and the language. "When he [Leonardo] arrived the first time, I really didn't know how he would handle the language," says Luhrmann. "After the initial read-through, we went through the text very thoroughly and deliberately and when we went back to it, the words just came out of his mouth as if it was the most natural language possible. To me, the language in Leonardo's mouth is a wonderful thing to hear because the words have resonance. He speaks them as if they really are his words, and that's something you don't always get in a Shakespearean performance."

"One of our main themes was clarity," says Claire. "During rehearsal, when Baz and Leo and I were working out what we were going to do, we did an exercise where we were absolutely literal. For every word we said, we'd find a way to make it clear with our hands. It was a little corny and we felt ridiculous doing it, but it really emphasized the idea that you can never be too obvious, precise, and clear with the language."

There were times when Claire didn't know how she was going to read the classic Shakespearean lines and bring new life to them. "I was sitting there about to go and do the famous balcony scene, and I was, like, 'What am I about to do? I'm about to say, "O, Romeo, Romeo! Wherefore art thou Romeo?" ' " she says. "And I'm thinking, 'This is a joke, right? How am I going to do this in a fresh way?' "

To say Leonardo was nervous about performing Shakespeare's language is an understatement. It didn't come easy to him at all. He wasn't sure, at first, how to play Romeo. "I thought I would have to put on an English accent and try a sort of Affected Shakespeare Thing," he says. "But Baz explained that he wanted to make it very understandable and clear, and after working with him awhile, I began to feel more comfortable with it. There is a lot of beauty in each word and when I began to dissect sentences, I'd find meanings referring to something way back in the script, or words with double and triple meanings. So I really had to know what I was talking about to do the words justice. But at the same time, I had to make it conversational. That was a challenge and different from anything I'd ever done—and I liked it."

Luhrmann's intention was to stay true to Shakespeare's play. As in the play, the first characters the audience meets are the Montague and Capulet gangs, with Tybalt (John Leguizamo) on the Capulets' side, and Mercutio (Harold Perrineau) on the Montagues' side. The Montagues (Brian Dennehy and Christina Pickles) and the Capulets (Paul Sorvino and Diane Venora) are rival crime syndicates. Romeo and Juliet live in a world of souped-up cars and designer guns. Leonardo says, "It's a much more wild, interesting version."

From the moment Romeo first sees Juliet through the glass of an aquarium at the Capulets' masked ball, the viewers know they are in for a visual masterpiece. Color became a big part of the filming of *Romeo & Juliet*. The photography is breathtaking, dominated by pale yellows and blues. As the two young lovers exchange their vows in a swimming pool, glowing shades of turquoise bounce off the water. Romeo wears mostly blue tones and silvers, while Juliet's signature color is pure white. Claire says of the film's style, "Everything was extreme, but not overdone. My eyes were constantly being fed."

William Shakespeare's Romeo & Juliet was originally going to be filmed on location in Miami, but the filmmakers decided to move the production to Mexico City for three wild months of shooting. *Romeo & Juliet* was shot in and around Mexico City, from Churubusco Studios to the barren badlands of Texcoco, from the middle of a fashionable shopping district to the beaches of Veracruz. All these locations collectively became Verona Beach.

From the moment the film company arrived in Mexico City, strange things began to happen. In the coastal village of Veracruz, where the death of Mercutio was filmed, cast and crew had to battle huge winds and killer bees.

Both Leonardo and Claire suffered from dysentery. Leonardo, who says he threw up for days, just kept praying, "Please don't let this happen. Let me get through this." He notes that "It was the *king* of Montezuma's revenge."

To cheer Leonardo up, a few of his friends flew in from New York to spend some time with him. One night Leonardo, his friends, and Claire decided to go out to a nightclub. It turned out to be a crazy night. The security guard at the club picked a fight with one of Leonardo's friends, and before anyone realized what had happened, his friend was on the ground bleeding, with broken ribs.

That same night, a crew member was hospitalized after a taxi he was in was hijacked by three men who slammed his head against the pavement and threatened to kill him if he didn't give them four hundred dollars. Claire remembers, "Everyone was getting stomped on that night." Leonardo says, "A lot of weird stuff happened that night. It must have been a full moon."

While the *Romeo & Juliet* set was far from perfect, Leonardo wasn't complaining. He found parts of the city interesting. "They say Mexico City has the worst smog of any city in the world. But it was nice too," he explains. "It's not a place where tourists tend to go. There's a lot of poverty, and that was depressing, but there are parts of the city that are just like Beverly Hills."

While he was in Mexico, he got excited about silver jewelry. "You can buy these bracelets, necklaces, and rings," he says. "They etch your name into them." Leonardo and a few other actors invested pretty heavily in silver jewelry. "We'd go out in the city wearing all this silver jewelry and people thought we were ridiculous," he says, laughing. "But they are nice things to have even though I haven't worn them since I got home."

Because the set consisted of a group of young Hollywood actors, a lot of partying went on between scenes. When the actors weren't spending their off time swimming in the hotel pool, they were videotaping their hotel room parties. "I think it was maybe a little more wild than it needed to be," admits Paul Rudd, who plays Paris, Juliet's other suitor.

Leonardo found he had fans in Mexico. Girls discovered that Leonardo was on the set and wanted to get a glimpse of him. Says John Leguizamo, "All the Mexican girls were going mad over him."

During filming, Leonardo found a way to keep himself, and others, from getting bored between takes: by doing Michael Jackson impersonations. When he got tired of that, he started imitating the rest of the cast as they struggled with the Shakespearean lines.

"I'd walk in front of the camera, and Leonardo would do my line all screechy, 'Thou or I must go,' " says Leguizamo. "So the next time I'd become really self-conscious. I just hated him, because it came so easy to that little blond, happy golden boy. He'd smoke a cigarette, do some laps, do Michael Jackson, go on the set, and there it was."

Claire found Leonardo "extremely funny. Sometimes I'd be doubled over in pain from laughing so hard. That was important especially when the scenes were intense. It was a real treat working with him."

At first, not everyone on the set found him as much fun to be around. But by the end of the shoot, the rest of the cast and crew got used to his impressions and jokes. "People say that Marlon Brando was a constant practical joker, and with Leo you might see thirty characters come out of him in a day," says Luhrmann. "A regular sport with Leonardo is to impersonate me in fairly cruel, uncompromising ways. But acting is playing, and all that fooling around is keeping him in a constant state of playing."

Leonardo was thoroughly pleased with the final cut of the film, and he enjoyed the challenge of playing Romeo. "He's still innocent in this version," he says. "At least, in the first half he is. Then Mercutio dies and Tybalt dies, and everything just goes wrong. I'm crying all the time in the last half of the film. I cry a lot in this movie.

"Our *Romeo & Juliet* is a little more hard-core and a lot cooler," he continues. "Because I wouldn't have done it if I'd had to jump around in tights. *Romeo & Juliet* is this classic story. It's about those things that carry you in a certain direction and you can't stop; like when people run off to Vegas and get married. That's the beauty of it. They both [Romeo and Juliet] were people who had guts."

Baz Luhrmann had attempted a seemingly impossible task: to mix Elizabethan poetry with a pounding score aimed at the MTV generation. For most critics and moviegoers, this combination worked beautifully. In its opening weekend, *William Shakespeare's Romeo & Juliet* was number one at the box office and earned $12 million, more than any other screen adaptation of a Shakespearean play since Zeffirelli's version of the tragedy in 1968.

William Shakespeare's Romeo & Juliet was a personal triumph for Leonardo. It placed him on the A list of actors and positioned him as a leading man for the first time in his career. Playing Romeo in Baz Luhrmann's inventive, frenetic film had turned Leonardo DiCaprio into a major star.

chapter 10

THE REAL LEO

What is Leonardo DiCaprio like in private? For one thing, he is refreshingly natural and down-to-earth. In interviews, he never shies away from any question. Sometimes he laughs while he talks, but he's also serious and determined and comes across as someone who is certain of what he wants. Leonardo is extremely friendly, honest, and willing to express his innermost feelings.

He has admitted that being a successful movie star is a tough business. He is aware of the dangers of sudden fame.

"I'm an ordinary guy," he says. He is still friends with the kids he grew up with. He likes the fact that his old friends didn't treat him differently when he began acting.

"I have a good group of friends, people I've accumulated over the years," he says. "Some I've known since elementary school, some I met recently. I really like to have sweet people around me. I like to get to know people. Just give me someone who's relaxed and cool to hang out with."

When he's offscreen, Leonardo loves playing basketball with his friends or going to parties. He likes to have a good time when he isn't working. And he refuses to let his fame consume his life.

"I won't stay cooped up in my hotel room," he says. "Most famous people don't go out. I don't want to become a strange person. I don't want to give up the life I already have. My career should adapt to me."

Leonardo has learned how to use his fame to his advantage. He tries to attend premieres when he has the time, and often attends fashion shows.

People who have worked with him love him. At the wrap party for *The Basketball Diaries*, one production assistant said, "I adore Leonardo. He is the nicest guy in the world."

Journalists have tried to turn Leonardo into the next James Dean or, more recently, the new River Phoenix, because of the tortured roles Leonardo has played onscreen. But he is not like either one of those actors, who gained fame too quickly and died too young.

Leonardo is sensitive, intelligent, and extremely well-mannered. He shrugs off all comparisons to other actors, although he likes the work of both James Dean and River Phoenix.

"My favorite James Dean film is *East of Eden.* That was his first film, and he was the best in it," says Leonardo. "Everyone always says *Rebel Without a Cause* was his best, but that was just too teenybopper for me."

As for River Phoenix, Leonardo will talk only about that actor's incredible performances. "I've always liked River's work," he explains. "I'm discounting the drugs and whatever he did in his personal life because the drugs weren't who he was. But as far as his acting and as far as who he was as a person, I respected him a lot. But I think I'm different from him."

Leonardo isn't much like the tormented characters he's played onscreen. He is a fun-loving guy who turns on serious emotions only for the cameras.

"I would have a nervous breakdown if I had to go through a movie for three months and be that character on and off the set," he says. "I know what I'm doing, but when they say, 'Cut,' I can joke around. I don't go hide in a corner and yell at anyone who tries to speak to me."

Far from being a Method actor, Leonardo, who has never taken an acting lesson, has found his own way to get into his characters.

"I know some actors get lost in what they're doing, but I'm not like that," he says. "I like to know everything that's going on around me. When I'm acting, I think of myself as the camera. I'm watching myself act. I'm trying to see how what I'm doing looks from the outside."

Leonardo was particularly annoyed by the rumor that he takes drugs. Not long after he finished *The Basketball Diaries*, his name started popping up in the gossip columns. Because of his rapid rise to fame at such a young age, it seemed as if some writers were trying to knock him down with unflattering stories. Leonardo is well aware of the fact that the tabloids have to make money and gossip columnists have to fill space, but he couldn't understand why they did it at his expense.

"I don't do drugs. I've never done drugs in my life," he says. "I'm just not interested. If any of my friends start doing drugs, they're going to hear about it from me."

Leonardo says he made *The Basketball Diaries* to show how destructive taking drugs is and to discourage young people from even considering it. "What people don't realize is that I did that movie because of the whole heroin craze," he says. "I'm not saying I was doing a 'Say No to Drugs' special or anything, but I wanted to help make some kind of statement *against* heroin."

While he tried to ignore the gossip about him, Leonardo was grieving over two unexpected deaths in his family. "My grandfather died in 1995. That was very depressing for me," he says. "And then my dog died, our family dog. It was like my year of misery."

It was also the year he decided to move out of his mother's house and get a place of his own. Wealth and fame changed little in Leonardo's life. But they did provide him and his mother with more comforts and more possessions. Leonardo has been able to afford a silver BMW coupe, and he has enjoyed fixing up his own place. He has also bought a new stereo and bookshelves. He loves to read.

Leonardo is comfortable where he is right now. But deep down he's concerned about being poor again. That's probably one reason he likes to get involved with charities. "I can't tell you what a fantastic feeling it is to give to a good cause," he says.

Leonardo has donated a lot of his time to charities. He has done everything from visiting sick children at a local Ronald McDonald House, to donating food and clothes to the homeless, to attending benefits that raise money to combat AIDS.

He is also serious about environmental issues. Leonardo has been trying for years to find a way to protect the environment. "I care about the environment, so I've read a lot of books and watched a few TV programs that have told me what I can do to help," he says. Leonardo's interest in the environment originated with his mother, who always recycled paper and conserved water while he was growing up.

His interest became even sharper when he read about the manatee problem in Florida a few years ago. Manatees were being hit by fishing boats and were dying. Leonardo donated money to try to save them.

Leonardo's success came at rocketlike speed, and many wonder if it has changed him. The answer is no. This energetic star knows how to separate his professional life from his personal one.

What has been the key to keeping things in perspective for Leonardo? He says it's very simple. "I know it is important to direct where you want to go with fame," he says. "But the main thing for me is to just maintain my life with my family and friends. They treat me like Leo, not like Leonardo, Master Thespian. That's all I need to maintain my sanity."

chapter 11

ROMANTIC RUMORS

With his ever-growing popularity, Leonardo has discovered that he can't avoid being linked romantically with actresses in the gossip columns. Every time he's seen with a pretty young woman, especially if she's also a star, the news reaches the papers that he's involved in a hot new romance.

Leonardo knows this kind of publicity comes with the territory. Since he can't escape and can't stop what's being written about him, he has learned to live with stories like these and shrug them off.

"I used to take everything to heart," he admits. "When the things they said about me in the press were detrimental, I thought it would kill me. But stuff keeps changing all the time, and now I'm cool about it, and I just think it's weird to watch it all happen."

One of the hottest items racing through the rumor mill was the story linking Leonardo with young actress Alicia Silverstone. Whether this rumor was true or false, it was splashed across newspapers and magazines for all the world to see. They said that the star of *Clueless* and *The Crush* had developed a *real* crush on Leonardo DiCaprio. And that the two stars were enjoying a secret relationship.

Was the story true? Leonardo and Alicia do know each other. In fact, when she first hit Hollywood, Leonardo was one of the first stars Alicia hung out with. But there were usually ten other people with them.

When Leonardo was asked about his so-called relationship with Alicia, he said in one magazine, "Alicia and I did our first movies at about the same time. We've known each other for years. I'm sure she was asked this question, and she thought it was ridiculous, and she just said, 'I'm not even going to answer that question,' just like I would do."

But that isn't what Alicia did. In fact, when she was asked about Leonardo, she went into detail about how she feels toward him, saying, "I think Leo is pretty cool."

At only eighteen years old, Alicia became an overnight sensation with the hugely popular film *Clueless*. But this star has had a hard time adjusting to her newfound success. Not long after gaining fame, Alicia decided to attend The Forum, a three-day self-help course that helps people deal with stress.

"When I first came to Hollywood, I trusted *everybody*. I'm a real people-pleaser," she says. "In my work I can *be* that sexy girl because I'm an actress, but it's not *me*. The Forum really helped me a lot with that stuff. And that's where I met Leo."

Leonardo also took the course; in fact, he went on to the advanced course of The Forum. He met a girl named Caitlin in the class and dated her briefly. Once or twice Leonardo, Caitlin, and Alicia all went out together after a Forum class to eat and talk.

With Leonardo's help, Alicia has been able to deal with her fame a little better. He's given her advice on how to handle show business pressures. That has been the extent of their "relationship"—they're just friends.

Another girl whom Leonardo claims he's just friends with is Chynna Phillips's half sister, the petite model Bijou. He's been seen with her all over New York City.

Leonardo has always been a favorite with members of the opposite sex. As far back as junior high school, girls have adored him. In eighth grade, he went on his very first date, which he says turned out to be a disaster and the first and last time he saw the girl.

"My first date was with this girl named

Cessi, this little Spanish beautiful girl," he says. "We had this beautiful relationship over the phone all summer. And then she came home, and we went to the movies for the first time. I wanted it to be so perfect. So I put on my light-blue turtleneck, which I thought was cool at the time. When I saw Cessi, I was petrified and I couldn't even look at her.

"We went to see *When Harry Met Sally* . . . and I couldn't move," Leonardo continues. "For two hours I was at peace because she was watching the movie. Then afterwards, I remember we went out to eat and ordered these French-dip sandwiches. The only thing I knew how to do was make fun of her and she got all freaked out. I remember she said, 'Do you have a problem with me eating this sandwich?' And that was our first and last date. I was in love with her for a year, but she wouldn't talk to me. Every two weeks she had library study, and I'd ditch class because that was the only place where I knew she'd be. But I couldn't go near her because I was so mortified."

Leonardo's first-kiss story isn't that much better. "I'll tell you about the first kiss I had," he says. "It was the most disgusting thing in my life. The girl injected about a pound of saliva into my mouth, and when I walked away I had to spit it all out. It was awful."

Despite his description of his first date and his first kiss, Leonardo is really a very romantic guy. When he is with someone he loves, he never lets a day go by without displaying his true feelings. Leonardo is always laughing and likes to be with someone who has a good sense of humor.

"I am the kind of guy who finds out what a girl likes and compliments them," says Leonardo, who enjoys taking long walks on the beach with the one he loves.

"I like girls who are intelligent," he says. "Someone funny and pretty—with a nice personality. Anyone I'm with has to give me my freedom. I like to be with someone who has character and style and someone who is very understanding."

Leonardo also believes in love at first sight. "You've got to keep the faith. Who doesn't like the idea that you could see someone tomorrow and she could be the love of your life? It's very romantic," he says.

Today, Leonardo ignites excitement everywhere he goes. He is adored by millions of young women in the United States and around the world. Many would love to meet him, give him a hug, and spend some time getting to know him better. Leonardo could have any girl he wants. Unfortunately, he just doesn't have the time. His filming schedules take him away for months at a time, so he's never in one place long enough to work on a relationship. But his love life remains strong. "It's been good," he says. "I haven't had my heart broken in a while."

At only twenty-three years old, Leonardo is not rushing into anything yet. He knows he has plenty of time for marriage in the future. "I definitely want to have the security of settling down someday. I'm looking forward to getting married and having kids," he confesses. "But it's not my time to do that right now."

chapter 12

RIDING A WAVE
OF SUCCESS

Leonardo DiCaprio is riding a wave of popularity and success that will crest only in the coming years.

Immediately after *Romeo & Juliet*, he signed on as one of the stars of *Marvin's Room*. The film, based on the successful play by Scott McPherson, gave Leonardo a chance to work with Meryl Streep, Diane Keaton, and Robert De Niro. Leonardo plays a rebellious and troubled teenager whose world is changed when he pays a visit to his aunt.

Some thought Leonardo was ready to tackle adult roles. But for the moment, he didn't mind playing younger parts, especially if it meant working with actors like De Niro, Streep, and Keaton. "People get into trouble trying to force themselves into adulthood," he says. "I'm still going to do whatever teenage roles I can. After all, I'll never be able to play those roles again."

In early 1996, Leonardo decided to do something he'd never done before: He accepted a role in a movie with a big budget and even bigger special effects. He agreed to join the cast of the eagerly anticipated *Titanic*. The film was to be directed by James Cameron, who filmed such box office smashes as *Aliens* and *The Terminator*. The budget for *Titanic* was $120 million.

Once again Leonardo journeyed to Mexico, where *Titanic* was shot. "We filmed some of it on Rosarito Beach," he says. "There was garbage everywhere. After living in Mexico for three months with *Romeo & Juliet* and six months with *Titanic*, I've spent nearly one year of my life there."

Being part of *Titanic* made Leonardo realize he'd like to branch out in the future and play as many diverse characters as possible.

There's no denying that Leonardo DiCaprio possesses the insight and natural ability to keep his career moving forward for many years to come. "I really enjoy acting," he says sincerely. "You just get the feeling all the time like you have to have more. And no matter how good it is, it's never enough. I think the public expects that from you. They want you to keep going, otherwise you could fade away. I love what I do and hope I can still be in this business in the future."

chapter 13

THE UNSINKABLE LEONARDO

With the release of *Titanic*, Leonardo sailed into superstardom. The most expensive movie in history—its final budget was $200 million—was originally slated for a summer 1997 release. When it finally hit theaters on December 17, 1997, the romantic, action-packed epic quickly took first place at the box office.

Leonardo's riveting performance as the film's sensitive hero earned him rave reviews. *Newsday* wrote, "DiCaprio has a captivating presence in a role that might have been written for a young Clark Gable." Leonardo was declared "the world's biggest heartthrob" by *Vanity Fair* magazine, and *People* named him one of the most intriguing people of the year. When the nominations for the Golden Globe Awards were announced, Leonardo had won a Best Actor nomination, and *Titanic* had received seven more nominations, including Best Picture.

It was already clear that Leonardo had easily made the transition from child actor to leading man. In fact, the studios were so eager to work with him that they proposed him to writer-director James Cameron for the lead role in *Titanic*. "The curious thing is, I actually didn't want Leo at first," says Cameron. "He didn't strike me as necessarily having the qualities I wanted. But I met him and basically just loved him. He can quickly charm a group of people without doing anything obvious. The second I met him I was convinced.

"I just felt you would care about him a lot more," Cameron continues. "He has tremendous vitality onscreen. Leo has a kind of wiry, survival quality about him that's pretty cool."

In *Titanic*, Leonardo plays Jack Dawson, a free-spirited artist who is coming back to the United States after spending several years in Europe. He wins his third-class ticket for the great ship's inaugural voyage in a poker game. As the ship sails, Jack meets a first-class passenger named Rose DeWitt Bukater (Kate Winslet), who is traveling home to Philadelphia with her mother, Ruth (Frances Fisher), and her fiancé, Caledon Hockley (Billy Zane). When Jack and Rose meet, the class lines that separate them blur. As Jack opens Rose's eyes to a world outside her wealthy circle, the two fall passionately in love.

Leonardo describes Jack as "a sort of wandering person who seizes on the opportunities life presents to him. At a young age I think he realizes how short life really is, and that's a big factor in who he is as a person."

In *Titanic,* Leonardo shows off more than his incredible acting ability. As part of their painstaking re-creation of the styles and manners of 1912, the filmmakers hired dialect coach Susan Hegarty to instruct the actors in behavior and speech. They also employed choreographer and etiquette coach Lynne Hockney. Leonardo worked closely with Hockney for his dancing scene with Rose.

"It was interesting," he says. "You have to accept it was a different time and they didn't have the same moves that are around now. It was a transition for me to get into it all. I actually joked around with my friends. I told them I did a little dancing in the movie. So I went to my room and made up a little routine that wasn't really what we were doing, and I sort of did a ballet. They just sat there in complete shock!"

At times Leonardo found etiquette training unnecessary for his character. "I worked with the etiquette coach," he says, "and halfway into it, I realized that in order to make Jack the character he is, he sort of needs to ignore such things. I'm supposed to stick out like a sore thumb in these environments. It was also very difficult to keep in mind the way things were said back then as we were improvising. Communication between men and women was different then. Jack disregards all that, and that's why Rose is interested in him."

Leonardo spent six months filming *Titanic* in Mexico. His work week sometimes lasted seventy hours, but he seemed to enjoy the process. The only thing he truly hated was climbing into the seventeen-million-gallon tank of water built for the movie. James Cameron jokes that half the shooting day was spent just getting Leonardo into the water.

Thinking back on that part of the filming, Leonardo says, "I know it's not really my cup of tea—all respect to Jim and the actors who do that type of thing." Everyone on the set knew how much Leonardo detested the water scenes. At the film's wrap party, Kate Winslet gave her costar a thermal blanket.

By the end of March 1997, Leonardo had wrapped the filming of *Titanic*. He was starting to miss his life in Los Angeles, but he wasn't ready to go home yet. Instead he decided to sign on as the star of Randall Wallace's remake of the Alexandre Dumas classic *The Man in the Iron Mask*. To play the dual role of Louis XIV and his brother, Philippe, Leonardo traveled to Paris for the filming. It was his first trip to France since filming *Total Eclipse,* and he was excited about taking on such a challenging acting project.

To prepare for the role, he got into terrific shape and learned to fence. "As an actor, you dream about being part of a movie like this," he said during production. "This film has it all. A great story and the perfect cast."

Leonardo's stirring performance breathes new life into the legendary tale. The film also stars John Malkovich, Gérard Depardieu, and Jeremy Irons as the Three Musketeers. Gabriel Byrne plays D'Artagnan.

The time Leonardo spent in France filming *The Man in the Iron Mask* was exhilarating for him. When he wasn't on the set, he was seeing the sights. His close friends Jonah Johnson, Tobey Maguire, and Ethan Suplee flew to the set to spend some time with him. "Usually Leo has in his contract that they have to give him plane tickets so he can have his friends come and hang out," says Jonah.

While in France, Leonardo realized that he was starting to be recognized more often on the street. On a trip he made to the Louvre, thirty screaming girls chased him, trying to rip the shirt off his back. For the rest of his time in France, groups of girls constantly collected outside his apartment, calling his name and trying to get a glimpse of him.

Despite the frenzy surrounding him, Leonardo hasn't changed at all. Claire Danes, his costar in *William Shakespeare's Romeo & Juliet,* says, "Leo's truly brilliant. He's in the center of this chaos, yet he carries himself really well." Leonardo has told one reporter, "I'm just trying to get used to all the attention."

Although he received his first million-dollar paycheck for *Titanic,* he remains frugal. His friend Ethan Suplee says, "Leo's cheap. I feel funny saying that, but I've said it to him. He'll look for a place in the street to park rather than use valet parking."

Leonardo enjoys buying computer and video equipment and is now planning to buy houses for both his mother and his father. His parents remain very important in his life. They are both fully involved in his career. According to Mark Wahlberg, "Leo has a lot of family support. They keep him sane."

Often Leo's mother and grandmother visit him on the sets of his films and at photo sessions. He will work with his father on a film project: George DiCaprio will be associate producer of a drama about the Julius and Ethel Rosenberg case in which Leonardo will star.

Leonardo insists he's going to take some time off, but he continues to accept interesting roles. In an upcoming Woody Allen movie, he will play a young Hollywood celebrity. He decided to take the small part because he wanted to work with Allen.

These are tremendously exciting days for Leonardo DiCaprio. He has proved his talents in one film after another, with more challenges and greater success sure to follow.

Producer Martin Brown, who worked with Leonardo on *William Shakespeare's Romeo & Juliet*, says, "He's intensely interesting to be around, very active and very much a live wire. He's astonishing." Meryl Streep, who costarred with Leonardo in *Marvin's Room*, says, "My kids think he's hot." Kate Winslet sums it up best when she describes Leonardo as "a natural."

Kate continues, "He's probably the world's most beautiful-looking man, yet he doesn't think he's gorgeous. He's the actor of the century. Nobody can get near him at this point!"

chapter 14

A Night to
Remember

There was excitement in the air on Sunday, January 18, 1998. It was the night of the 55th Golden Globe Awards, and *Titanic* had captured eight nominations. The street in front of the ritzy Beverly Hilton Hotel in Beverly Hills, California, was lined with eager fans, photographers, and reporters.

The Golden Globe Awards, which honor excellence in movies and television, have become a glamorous, star-studded event. In fact, more stars go to the Golden Globe Awards than to the Academy Awards.

With all Hollywood's royalty in attendance, it was Leonardo DiCaprio who drew the loudest screams from the audience. The crowds were chanting his name even before he arrived. When a reporter walked over to a group of fans and asked who they were waiting for, the answer came back in unison: "We love Leo!"

Finally the wait was over. Leonardo emerged

from a long, shiny limousine and was greeted by a barrage of camera and TV lights. He flashed his winning smile, then immediately walked over to the fans and waved.

Every person who met Leonardo that night agrees that he was as nice as everyone says. His sudden burst of fame hadn't gone to his gorgeous head. He was still as down-to-earth as he had been before he became a star. Fans concurred: Success couldn't have happened to a more deserving person.

He arrived with his *Titanic* costar Kate Winslet on his arm. The two stars looked stunning together, and they graciously stopped and posed for the cameras. They spoke with reporters and signed autographs for fans. They were the talk of the Golden Globe Awards.

As Leonardo and Kate walked down the long red carpet, people wondered if they were Hollywood's newest romantic couple. Kate just laughed as Leonardo answered everyone's questions.

Entertainment Tonight's Bob Goen asked Leonardo if he and Kate had come together. "Yes, we came together," said Leonardo with a smile. "But we're just good buddies."

Another reporter wanted to know how Leonardo felt about being named Hollywood's hot new heartthrob. "Well, it isn't a label I placed on myself," Leonardo answered. "But it's great. I'm really proud to be part of a film like *Titanic*."

Out of the eight nominations, *Titanic* won four Golden Globe Awards. Composer James Horner won for Best Original Score. The film's song, "My Heart Will Go On," was named Best Original Song. James Cameron was named Best Director. And *Titanic* was named Best Dramatic Movie.

When he accepted the award for Best Dramatic Movie, James Cameron pulled Leonardo and Kate up to the podium with him. He just felt he couldn't accept the award without his two stars standing next to him. When he got to the microphone, he said, "Leo and Kate are the center of this picture."

Backstage, Leonardo looked a little dazed by the thrilling evening. He told reporters, "This has been an exciting night for *Titanic*." The fact that Leonardo hadn't won an award himself didn't seem to faze him. He was thrilled for everyone else who took home a Golden Globe Award, especially everyone connected with *Titanic*.

As far as the journalists were concerned, Leonardo was the evening's biggest star. Asked how he feels about his success, he told one reporter, "This has been the most phenomenal time in my life. It's been like catching my breath. I never expected all this. It's been incredible!"

When the Golden Globe Awards show ended, the night was just beginning for Leonardo. As he arrived at one of the after-parties, crowds of fans followed him. The Oscar buzz was humming around Leonardo and *Titanic*, but he wasn't thinking about that. *Titanic* had taken home four Golden Globe Awards, and that was all that mattered to him. For Leonardo, it was certainly a night to remember.

leonardo's vital statistics

Full real name: Leonardo Wilhelm DiCaprio

Nicknames: Leo, The Noodle

Birthdate: November 11, 1974

Birthplace: Hollywood, California

Current residence: Hollywood, California

Height: 6 feet

Weight: 140 pounds

Hair color: Blond

Eye color: Blue green

Parents' names: George and Irmelin DiCaprio

Favorite book: *The Old Man and the Sea* by Ernest Hemingway

Favorite sports: Basketball, baseball

Favorite musician: Harry Connick, Jr.

Favorite bands: Pink Floyd, The Beatles, Led Zeppelin

Favorite actors: Robert De Niro, Al Pacino, Jack Nicholson

Favorite actress: Meg Ryan

Favorite TV show: *The Twilight Zone*

Favorite vacation place: Germany

Favorite food: Pasta

Favorite drink: Lemonade

Favorite colors: Black, purple

Favorite childhood memory: Terrorizing his neighborhood with practical jokes

Favorite cities: New York, San Francisco

Favorite movies: The three *Godfather* films

Habits: "Twisting my hair and biting my nails"

Musical instrument played: "I used to play the organ."

Biggest wishes: To save the environment and live in peace

Best birthday: "My sixteenth because I started to drive."

Little-known fact: He speaks German fluently.

Childhood description: "Funny, goofy, and cute"

Best quality: "I have a good sense of humor."

Worst quality: He procrastinates.

Main goal in life: To be a successful actor

did you know . . . ?

When he was a child, people mistook Leonardo for a girl because of his long blond hair and the outfits he was dressed in. Says his mother, Irmelin DiCaprio, "I would make little red velvet outfits and my mother would send me different-colored shoes from Germany for Leo to wear. In those days, boys didn't have fancy clothes, and he would argue with me about how I'd try to dress him."

When Leonardo is asked to describe himself, he says, "I'm shy, but when the time comes to be wild, I am. I'm fun-loving, adventurous, and mysterious."

His first memory is of wearing red-and-yellow tap shoes and being lifted onto a stage by his father to entertain people waiting for a concert.

Leonardo is serious about social issues such as taking care of the environment and helping the homeless.

Juliette Lewis, who costarred with Leonardo in *What's Eating Gilbert Grape* and *The Basket-*

ball Diaries, affectionately calls him "my little pal."

Leonardo is a big fan of the Los Angeles Lakers basketball team. "I absolutely refuse to miss a Lakers game," he says. "They are great ball-players and fascinating to watch."

Whenever he has time off, Leonardo makes his own videos starring his friends.

Leonardo likes to chew "chewing tobacco" bubble gum and drink Fruitopia.

He has a large supply of five-dollar sunglasses in all shapes and sizes.

Leonardo drives a silver BMW coupe.

Leonardo spent the summer of 1996 in amusement parks. "I had my ultra–amusement park summer," he says. "I went to Knott's Berry Farm, Magic Mountain, Raging Waters, and Universal Studios three times."

"I like to do things that scare me," says Leonardo. He recently took up river rafting, scuba diving, bungee jumping, and skydiving. His first skydiving trip almost turned deadly when his parachute failed to open. He had to free-fall until his backup chute opened. Of the experience, he says, "The whole trip down I didn't cry. I was just depressed."

When he is asked if success has spoiled him, Leonardo says, "No. I'm handling it well. I haven't gone crazy yet."

Where will Leonardo be in ten years? "I'll probably be acting," he says. "But if I get tired of it, I may go into directing. I'm interested in staying in the movie business."

filmography

CRITTERS 3 (1991)
Directed by: Kristine Peterson
Cast: Leonardo DiCaprio, Christopher
   Cousins, Joseph Cousins, Don Opper

POISON IVY (1992)
Directed by: Katt Shea Ruben
Produced by: Andy Ruben
Screenplay by: Katt Shea Ruben, Andy Ruben
Music by: Aaron Davies
Released by: New Line Cinema

Cooper	Sara Gilbert
Ivy	Drew Barrymore
Darryl	Tom Skerritt
Georgie	Cheryl Ladd
Guy #1	Leonardo DiCaprio

THIS BOY'S LIFE (1993)
Directed by: Michael Caton-Jones
Produced by: Art Linson
Screenplay by: Robert Getchell
Director of Photography: David Watkin
Based on the book by: Tobias Wolff

Music by: Carter Burwell
Released by: Warner Brothers

Dwight Hansen	Robert De Niro
Caroline Wolff	Ellen Barkin
Tobias Wolff	Leonardo DiCaprio
Arthur Gayle	Jonah Blechman

WHAT'S EATING GILBERT GRAPE (1993)

Directed by: Lasse Hallström
Produced by: Meir Teper, Bertil, David Matalon
Screenplay by: Peter Hedges, based on his novel
Director of Photography: Sven Nykvist, A.S.C.
Music by: Alan Parker, Bjorn Isfalt
Released by: Paramount Pictures

Gilbert Grape	Johnny Depp
Arnie Grape	Leonardo DiCaprio
Becky	Juliette Lewis
Betty Carver	Mary Steenburgen
Momma	Darlene Cates
Amy Grape	Laura Harrington
Ellen Grape	Mary Kate Schellhardt
Mr. Carver	Kevin Tighe

THE FOOT SHOOTING PARTY (1994)

Leonardo was the star of this twenty-minute short film. It was released by Touchstone Pictures, and the executive producer was Renny Harlin.

THE QUICK AND THE DEAD (1995)
Directed by: Sam Raimi
Produced by: Joshua Donen, Allen Shapiro, Patrick Markey
Coproduced by: Sharon Stone, Chuck Binder
Written by: Simon Moore
Director of Photography: Dante Spinotti
Music by: Alan Silvestri
Released by: TriStar Pictures

Ellen	Sharon Stone
Herod	Gene Hackman
Cort	Russell Crowe
Kid	Leonardo DiCaprio
Eugene Dred	Kevin Conway
Marshall	Gary Sinise

THE BASKETBALL DIARIES (1995)
Directed by: Scott Kalvert
Produced by: Liz Heller, John Bard Manulis
Screenplay by: Bryan Goluboff
Based on the book by: Jim Carroll
Music by: Graeme Revell
Released by: New Line Cinema

Jim Carroll	Leonardo DiCaprio
Jim's Mother	Lorraine Bracco

Mickey	Mark Wahlberg
Pedro	James Madio
Neutron	Patrick McGaw
Swifty	Bruno Kirby
Reggie	Ernie Hudson
Diane	Juliette Lewis
Skinhead	Michael Rapaport

TOTAL ECLIPSE (1995)
Directed by: Agnieszka Holland
Produced by: Jeane-Pierre Ramsay Levi
Screenplay by: Christopher Hampton
Director of Photography: Yorgos Arvanitis
Music by: Jan A.P. Kaczmarek
Released by: Fine Line Features

Arthur Rimbaud	Leonardo DiCaprio
Paul Verlaine	David Thewlis
Mathilde Verlaine	Romane Bohringer
Isabelle Rimbaud	Dominique Blanc
Rimbaud's Mother	Nita Klein
Frédéric	James Thieree
Vitalie	Emmanuelle Oppo

WILLIAM SHAKESPEARE'S ROMEO & JULIET (1996)
Directed by: Baz Luhrmann
Produced by: Gabriella Martinelli, Baz Luhrmann
Screenplay by: Craig Pearce, Baz Luhrmann

Director of Photography: Donald M.
    McAlpine, A.S.C.
Music by: Nellee Hooper
Released by: 20th Century Fox

Romeo	Leonardo DiCaprio
Juliet	Claire Danes
Tybalt	John Leguizamo
Fulgencio Capulet	Paul Sorvino
Ted Montague	Brian Dennehy
Caroline Montague	Christina Pickles
Dave Paris	Paul Rudd
Gloria Capulet	Diane Venora
Mercutio	Harold Perrineau
Diva	Des'ree
Father Laurence	Pete Postlethwaite
Peter	Pedro Altamirano

MARVIN'S ROOM (1996)
Directed by: Jerry Zaks
Produced by: Robert De Niro, Jane Rosenthal,
    Scott Rudin, Adam Schroeder
Based on the play by: Scott McPherson
Released by: Miramax Films

Hank	Leonardo DiCaprio
Lee	Meryl Streep
Bessie	Diane Keaton
Dr. Wally	Robert De Niro
Marvin	Hume Cronyn
Ruth	Gwen Verdon

TITANIC (1997)

Directed by: James Cameron
Produced by: James Cameron, Jon Landau,
    Rae Sanchini
Screenplay by: James Cameron
Released by: 20th Century Fox/Paramount
    Pictures

Jack Dawson	Leonardo DiCaprio
Rose DeWitt Bukater	Kate Winslet
Cal Hockley	Billy Zane
Molly Brown	Kathy Bates
Brock Lovett	Bill Paxton
Rose Dawson Calvert	Gloria Stuart
Ruth DeWitt Bukater	Frances Fisher

THE MAN IN THE IRON MASK (1998)

Directed by: Randall Wallace
Produced by: Randall Wallace, Russ Smith,
    René Dupont
Screenplay by: Randall Wallace
Inspired by the classic French novel by:
    Alexandre Dumas
Director of Photography: Peter Suschitzky
Costume Designer: James Acheson
Released by: United Artists
Starring: Leonardo DiCaprio, Jeremy Irons,
John Malkovich, Gérard Depardieu, Gabriel
Byrne, Anne Parillaud, Judith Godreche

TELEVISION APPEARANCES

Leonardo appeared in fifteen commercials for Matchbox Cars, bubble gum, toys, and cereal

Mickey's Safety Club (educational film)

How to Deal with a Parent Who Takes Drugs (educational film)

Lassie (guest appearance)

The Outsiders (guest appearance)

Santa Barbara (daytime drama)

A Circus Fantasy (guest appearance)

Roseanne (guest appearance)

Parenthood (series; Leonardo played Garry Buckman)

Growing Pains (series; Leonardo played Luke Brower in the show's 1991–92 season)

About the Author

Grace Catalano is the author of two *New York Times* best-sellers: *New Kids on the Block* and *New Kids on the Block Scrapbook.* Her other books include biographies of Brad Pitt, Joey Lawrence, Jason Priestly, Paula Abdul, Gloria Estefan, Richard Grieco, Fred Savage, River Phoenix, Alyssa Milano, and Kirk Cameron. She is also the author of *Teen Star Yearbook,* which includes minibiographies of eighty-five celebrities. Grace Catalano has edited numerous magazines, including *Rock Legend, Star Legend, The Movie Times, CountryBeat, Country Style,* and the teen magazine *Dream Guys.* She and her brother, Joseph, wrote and designed *Elvis: A Tenth Anniversary Tribute, Elvis and Priscilla,* and *Country Music's Hottest Stars.* Grace Catalano lives on the North Shore of Long Island.